MW01141498

Mr. Pearse's Last Legacy. Two Discourses, (viz.) I. A Beam of Divine Glory

Mr. Pearse's *Last Legacy.*

TWO
DISCOURSES,
(*VIZ.*)

I. A Beam of Divine Glory:

OR,

The Unchangeableness of God Opened,
Vindicated, and Improved.

II. The Soul's Rest in God.

Very useful to quiet the Minds of Chri-
stians, when discomposed on the Account of Man's Mortality, and the
Mutability of Humane Affairs.

By E. P. Author of *The Great Concern:*
Or, *Preparation for Death,* &c.

The Third Edition. Price 1 *s.* Bound.

LONDON:

Printed for *J.* Robinson, at the *Golden
Lion* in St. *Paul's* Church-Yard, and
B. Aylmer, at the *Three Pigeons* in
Cornhill. 1704.

THE
PUBLISHERS
TO THE
READER.

THE Author of this and Two other
Treatises, Intituled, *The Beſt Match*,
and *The Great Concern: Or, Preparation
for Death*, did in a moſt Solemn manner (and with an intire Submiſſion to
the Divine Will) pray on his Death-Bed,
that in as much as his Days were ſhortned, God would be pleaſed to give his
Bleſſing to ſome Writings of his, that
they may Preach to, and do Good to the
Souls of Men (of which he was a great
Lover) when he was dead and gone, and
God was pleaſed to hear his Prayer, as
Thouſands can witneſs, into whoſe Hands
his Books are fallen.

This Treatiſe of the *Unchangeableneſs
of God* may well attend and be reckoned
a Second Part, or, Application of his
Book of Death: For when a Chriſtian is
made ſad on the Conſideration of Man's

Mortality, and the Mutability of all things under the Sun, what can better compose his Thoughts than the serious Contemplation of *God's Unchangeable-ness?* What is fittest for him to do when his Soul is full of Agitations on the Account of Changes here below, than to take up his *Rest in God,* who is *the Father of Lights, with whom is no variableness, neither Shadow of turning?* The Psalmist makes this Use of it; the whole *90th* Psalm seems to be Penned on this Account, (to which we refer the Reader) and Part of the *102d* Psalm, especially the *11th* Verse, where he thus declares his Sense of his Mortality.

My Days are like a Shadow that declineth, and I am withered like Grass.

But in the *11th* Verse he thus quiets his Mind, *But thou, O Lord, shalt endure for ever, and thy Remembrance unto all Generations.* As if he should have said, This is our Comfort, tho' we die and fall into the Dust, yet our God is Eternal, *And this is Life Eternal, to know him the only true God,* &c.

That God would be pleased to give the like Success to This as he hath to the former Treatises, is the Prayer of

J. R. B. A

T O

TO THE

READER.

THE Unchangeableſs of God *is one of thoſe Perfections of his whereby he is in a peculiar manner diſtinguiſhed from the* Creatures. *The Creatures are made up of Changes. Their* Beings, Life, Conditions, *are ſubject to many Changes. But God knows none of theſe Changes, his Being is moſt immutable, his Life the moſt even, conſtant, uniform, ſerene Life; his Happineſs at all times alike and the ſame.* God doth always abide in the ſame Likeneſs, 'Αεί μένει ἐν ὁμοία. *ſays one of the Ancients,* Philo Judæus. with him there is no Variableneſs, nor Shadow of Change. *Now there is an Inſtinct in us whereby we are carried out to deſire Unchangeableneſs. Every thing doth naturally deſire its Perfection; Man therefore being a reaſonable Creature, finding himſelf ſubject to many Changes, longs after a Perfect State, which is to be Unchangeable he would fain come to an Unchangeable Life, to an Unchangeable Happineſs. Now what*

he

To the Reader.

we cannot find or attain unto in our selves, we should aspire after by attaining Union and Conjunction with our Maker. Every thing is made perfect by reaching or attaining its First Cause or Principle. God is the Fountain of Life, the Fountain of Unchangeableness, so far as Unchangeableness is communicable to the Creatures. Indeed, in a strict and proper Sense Unchangeableness is one of the Incommunicable Attributes of God; none but God is simply and absolutely Unchangeable, or can be so. It implies a Contradiction to suppose a Creature, and that Creature intrinsecally and in its own Nature not to be under a Possibility of Change: but yet after a sort the Creatures may be made Unchangeable, in having an Unchangeable Life, an Unchangeable Happiness, given to them by some kind of Participation of God, who is the Chief Good, and who hath all Life and Happiness in himself. Thus the Holy Angels, who are not simply and absolutely Unchangeable in themselves, do yet enjoy an Unchangeable Life and Happiness in way of Donation and Communication, by the Sight of God, and Communion with God. We should therefore aspire after the Sight of God, and press after the most perfect Adherence to him. God only is the Centre of Unchangeableness, and by fixing our Hearts in him, we shall, after a sort, become Unchangeable. Joyn thy Heart to Eternity, (says Austin) and thou thy self shalt be Eternal.

The Author of the following Discourses hath now blessed Experience what that Partici-

pated

pated Unchangeableneſs *is*, (*if we may ſo call it*) *which Glorified Souls have in the Divine Preſence, by having* Communion *with God, the* Firſt Unchangeable Being. *Whilſt he lived here on Earth he ſaw many* Changes *paſſing over himſelf, both as to his Perſon and* Condition ; *this put him upon the Contemplation of the Unchangeableneſs of God, and cauſed him to ſeek for that Reſt in God which he could not find in himſelf, nor in any thing here below. And as thoſe that obſerved his Spirit did clearly perceive that he was much quickned and helped, as to his Spiritual Eſtate, by meditating much of an Holy Reſt in God ; ſo it is not to be doubted, if we take the ſame Courſe, and keep the Eye of our Minds fix d on God, labouring to take up all our Reſt and Satisfaction in him, there ſhall we find that true Quiet to our Souls which we vainly ſeek after in the Variety of Objects here below. And the ſerious peruſing of theſe Diſcourſes, which carry much of the Impreſs of the Author's Spirit upon them, may be of good Uſe to us to help us to attain ſuch an End.*

The Author *had no Thoughts at firſt of bringing forth theſe Sermons unto* Publick View, *but being much perſuaded hereunto by his Neareſt Relation, at laſt he yielded unto that Importunity, and perfected them with his own Hand. The reſt of his Notes being left in Characters, it is much to be feared theſe are the laſt Sermons of his that are like to ſee the Light.*

To the Reader.

For a Cloſe I may only add this, That it is matter of ſad Lamentation *to us, to conſider how many of the Faithful Servants of God, who have been* Eminent *in their Generations, have been taken away in a few Years. Certainly it becomes-us to bewail greatly the Deaths of ſo many* Godly Miniſters; *and ſince the Harveſt is great, and the Faithful Labourers are but few, we ſhould pray the Lord of the Harveſt that he would thruſt forth Labourers into the Vineyard.*

Thine in the Lord Chriſt,

JOHN ROWE.

A

A

Beam of Divine Glory:

O R,

The Unchangeableneſs of God, Aſſerted, Opened, Vindicated, and
Improved, from

Mal. 3. 6. *I am the Lord, I change not ;
therefore ye Sons of* Jacob *are not
conſumed.*

C H A P. I.

*Wherein way is made to the Text, the
Words thereof opened, the Foundation
of our intended Diſcourſe laid, and the
Principal Matters to be conſidered, in
the Proſecution of it, hinted at.*

IT is a great, as well as a true, Obſervation which
I have read in a Learned Man ; namely, That
all the many various Attributes of God mentioned in

*   the

the Scripture, are no other than his very Essence, *and are ascribed to him to help us in our Conceptions and Understandings of him,* who are not able to apprehend wh t may be known of God, *under any one Name or Notion,* or by any one *Act of the Intellect.* We read (you know) of his Power, his Wisdom, his Holiness, his Justice, his Goodness, his Faithfulness, his All-sufficiency, and the like, all which are not distinguished in him, either from himself, or from one another, but are all one and the same God revealed and manifested to us, under various Notions, and that to help us the better to conceive and apprehend him, as also to perform our Homage and Worship to him ; accordingly we may say, the Holiness of God is God; the Wisdom of God is God, the Power of God is God ; the Goodness of God is God : And to come to my Text, the Unchangeableness of God is God ; and indeed the Unchangeableness of God is God manifested and revealed under a Sweet and Blessed, as well as a Glorious, Notion to us, under such a Notion as conduces much to the quickning and incouraging of our Faith and Love, our Comfort and Obedience in him, and to him, and so indeed the Text represents it, *I am the Lord, I change not, therefore ye Sons of Jacob are not consumed :* In which Words we have Two Things to be noted.

1. Here is a Display or Representation of God in one Ray or Beam of his Divine Glory, and that is his Unchangeableness, *I am the Lord, I change not ,* or, I the Lord am not changed: For it may be read either Actively or Passively, and the Sense will be the same . *I change not,* I am not alter'd or varied at all ; what I was I am, what I am I still shall be : *God here* (as a Judicious Expositor observes,) *tacitly opposes himself to mortal Men, and removes and renounces all Wavering and Inconstancy from himself. I change not ,* as if he should have said,

Men

Men die, but I live; Men change, but I change not, I am still the same.

2. Here is a Mention or Declaration of the Blessed Fruit or issue of this Glorious Perfection of God, in Reference to his Church and People, and that is their Preservation from Destruction: *Therefore ye Sons of* Jacob *are not consumed.* Here Two Things must be enquired into; First, Who are we to understand by the Sons of *Jacob?* And Secondly, What by their being not consumed?

1. Who are we to understand by the Sons of *Jacob?* By the Sons of *Jacob* here we are to understand God's Professing Church and People. We read in Scripture of *the House of* Jacob, *the Seed of* Jacob, *and the Sons of* Jacob; by all which are meant God's Church and People, whom he takes into Covenant with himself, and makes the Objects of his Love; and this will be evident by comparing my Text with *Cap.* 1. 2. where God says expresly that *he loved them*; and again, *I loved* Jacob.

2. What are we to understand by their being not consumed? It imports and carries in it these Two Things.

    1. An Exemption from Temporal Ruin.

    2. A Preservation from Eternal Destruction.

1. An Exemption from Temporal Ruin: *Therefore ye are not consumed:* That is, Therefore you are not cut off from being a People; therefore you are not utterly broken by my Judgments; 'tis true, some Afflictions you have had, yea, great Afflictions; but yet still you live, still you are a People, you are preserved from utter Ruin and Destruction. And why so? Not because you have not deserved to be utterly cut off and destroyed, but because I am unchangeable; *I am the Lord, I*

change

change not; *therefore ye Sons of* Jacob *are not con-*
fumed.

2. A Prefervation from Eternal Deftruction;
Therefore ye are not confumed; that is, therefore
you are not in Hell, therefore you are not under
the Eternal Revelations of my Wrath, which
(alas!) is what you have deferved : As if God
fhould fay to them, True, you have had Affliction,
but (alas!) it has been nothing to the defert of your
Sin, your Sins have been many and great againft
me, fuch as deferved utter Ruin, yea, eternal
Deftruction, and utter Confumption both of Body
and Soul for ever; and this had been your Portion long fince, had you not had to deal with an
unchangeable God; not your Defert, but my unchangeablenefs is the fole Caufe why you are not
utterly and eternally deftroyed.

In fhort, the Defign of the whole was to
upbraid them with their Sins, and particularly their Ingratitude; and withal to let them
know, that the Reafon why it was not worfe
with them than it was, yea, why they were not
totally and eternally deftroyed, was not becaufe
they did not deferve to have had it fo, but becaufe their God was unchangeable : *I am the Lord,*
I change not; *therefore, &c.* In which God feems
thus to befpeak them : You complain of me, and
have hard Thoughts of me, becaufe 'tis with you
as it is, and I do not prefently arife for your
Help; but let me tell you, 'tis well for you that
'tis not ten thoufand times worfe with you than it
is; 'tis well you are a People; 'tis well you are
not among the Damned; fure I am *you highly*
deferv'd to have had it fo with *you* : You are a
finful, finning, rebellious People, a People that
have deferved to be deftroyed Ten thoufand times
over; I have done great things for you above any
People, I have fhewn you much Love, but you
have

have not walked ſuitably and anſwerably to the
great things I have done for you, nor the great
Love I have ſhewn to you: No, you have abuſed
all, and ſinned againſt me under all, and that with
an High Hand, whereby you have deſerved to be
utterly conſumed and deſtroyed; and indeed, had
I not been an unchangeable God, conſum'd and
deſtroyed you had been long ago; I ſee that in
you and among you for which I might juſtly deſtroy you, and that for ever, and nothing but my
own unchangeableneſs keeps you alive; ſhould you
therefore complain of me! Should you not rather
admire at my Patience and Forbearance ſo long
with you ? Truly 'tis a Miracle of Grace, Goodneſs and Patience in me, that you have not been
long ſince deſtroyed once for all. This I take to
be the true Scope and Meaning of the Word; the
Sum of which, together with the Foundation of
my intended Diſcourſe from them, I ſhall give you
in this ſhort Poſition; namely,

That the Lord Jehovah is an unchangeable God;
or how changeable ſoever the Creatures are,
yet God the Lord changes not.

Whoever changes, I the Lord change not, I am
always and for ever the ſame. Now that God is
unchangeable, wherein he is unchangeable, why
or whence 'tis that he is unchangeable, as alſo the
Vindication of his Unchangeableneſs from all Cavils and Objections that ſeem to lye againſt it,
with the Practical Improvement of all, are the
Principal Matters that will fall under Conſideration
in the Proſecution of this Argument; and I hope,
by the Aſſiſtance of God, we ſhall find ſome Light
and much Comfort and Quickening in our going
through them.

CHAP.

CHAP. II.

Which contains a general Proof of the Unchangeableness of God.

THE Creatures, yea, the best of Creatures in themselves are subject to change ; but God is every way, and in all respects, unchangeable, God himself expresly here (you see) asserts his own Unchangeableness. *I am the Lord, I change not ;* and 'tis frequently asserted also elsewhere, *Jam.* 1. 17. *Every good and perfect Gift,* (says the Apostle) *cometh down from above, from the, Father of Lights, with whom is no Variableness or Shadow of Change.* God is here called *the Father of Lights.* He is sometimes called *Light* it self, 1 *John* 1. 5. *God is Light.* By which (as a Learned Man observes) *is noted to us the Majesty, Holiness, and perfect Blessedness of God* ; and here he is called 'the *Father of Lights.* To note that all Light, all Glory, all Holiness and Blessedness, is originally in him, and that whatever of these Creatures do partake of, does come from him as its proper Spring and Fountain. Now with this Father of Lights there is (says the Apostle) *no Variableness,* no Mutation ; the Word is παραλλαγὴ, which is an Astronomical Term taken from the Heavenly Bodies, which suffer many Declinations and Revolutions ; the Heavenly Lights have their Vicissitude and Eclipses, their Decreases and Increases ; but with God, *the Father of Lights,* there is no such thing, he always shines with a like Brightness, Lustre, and Glory, *with whom is no variableness, nor Shadow of turning* ; that is, he is without the least Shew or Resemblance of Change ; nothing that looks like a

Change

Change is found in him : God is a Sun which doth not Set and-Rife, that can never be Overcaſt or Eclipſed. So alſo, *Pſal.* 102. 24, 25, 26, 27. *I ſaid, O my God, take me not away in the midſt of my Days, thy Years are throughout all Generations : Of old haſt thou laid the Foundations of the Earth, and the Heavens are the Work of thy Hands; they all periſh, but thou ſhalt endure, all of them ſhall wax old like a Garment, as a Veſture ſhalt thou change them, and they ſhall be changed. But thou art the ſame, and thy Years ſhall have no End.* Pray obſerve, the Heavens are the pureſt Part of the Creation, yet they, the *Pſalmiſt* tells us, *ſhall wax old, and be changed*, but ſays he to God, *thou art the ſame, and thy Years ſhall have no End*; thou changeſt not, but what thou wert thou art, and wilt be ſo for ever. The Heavens, and ſo all the Creatures, do not only wax old and change; but obſerve, they *change and wax old like a Garment.* Cloth by Degrees will rot, and be eaten out by Moths, but a Garment or Veſture is worn and waſted every Day; every Day brings Changes upon the Creatures more or leſs, but God changes not, he remains the ſame for ever ; *from Everlaſting to Everlaſting he is God,* as you have it, *Pſal.* 90. 2. that is, he is unchangeably one and the ſame infinitely Holy and Bleſſed One. *God* (ſays one of the Ancients) *who changes all things, who works all the Changes are in the World, is himſelf unchangeable, never New, never Old.* Thus you ſee that God is unchangeable. Now if you ask me what this Unchangeableneſs of God is ? I anſwer, that 'tis that Attribute of God whereby he is free from all Corruption and Alteration, is always like himſelf, ſo as that he can neither ceaſe to be what he is, nor begin to be what he is not; and hereby he is infinitely diſtinguiſhed from all the Creatures in Perfection and Glory: They are all ſubject to Corruption and Alteration; at leaſt in
their

their own Nature they are so, if not in their Condition; they may ceafe to be what they are, and may begin to be what they are not, they may lofe what they had, and may attain fomewhat which before they had not; even the very Angels themfelves are in themfelves thus mutable, as may be more fully hereafter fhewn. But now with God there is no fuch thing, he is free from all Poffibility of Corruption or Alteration; he is always the fame, nor can he ceafe to be what he is, or begin to be what he is not. But that God is unchangeable, and alfo what his Unchangeablenefs is, will further appear by what next falls under Confideration.

C H A P. III.

Which fhews wherein, in a peculiar manner, God is unchangeable.

HAving thus given you a general Proof of God's unchangeablenefs, our next Work fhall be to confider wherein he is unchangeable; by which we fhall be both further enlightned and confirmed in this Truth, and withal brought, I hope, into an Acquaintance with the Life, Power, and Sweetnefs of it, at leaft in fome Meafure. God then is unchangeable, efpecially in Six things, all which do carry unexpreffible Sweetnefs, as well as Glory in them, and fhould be great Encouragements to our Faith and Comfort. He is unchangeable,

1. In his being an Effence.
2. In his Bleffednefs and Glory.

3. In

3. In his Council and Decree.
4. In his Kingdom and Rule.
5. In his Covenant and Promiſe.
6. In his Love and Grace to his People.

1. God is unchangeable in his Being and Eſſence. What the Being or Eſſence of God is, is not eaſie for us to conceive or apprehend ; the Learned tell us, that the Eſſence or Being of God is that one meer and pure Act whereby God is God; or thus, that *God, in reſpect of his Eſſence, is one moſt pure and meer Act from which all things are, and to which all things return*, that is, which is the Firſt Cauſe and and the Laſt End of all things. But whatever the Eſſence or Being of God is, yet to be ſure he is therein unchangeable, he cannot be changed into another Eſſence or Being, nor can that which he hath, or rather is, be corrupted or decay: So much is held forth in my very Text. God therein ſtiling himſelf *Jehovah*. Which Name or Title of his notes, as the Truth and Abſoluteneſs, ſo the Sameneſs and Unchangeableneſs of his Being: Thus *Calvin* and others note upon the Place, and therefore do make that [*I change not*] to be but an *Exegeſis*, or ſomewhat added by way of Explication of this Title *Jehovah*, which here God gives himſelf, *I am Jehovah, I change not*; *q. d.* I am an Abſolute, Independent, Unchangeable Being in my ſelf, and one that gives Being to all the Creatures ; and thus the Learned in the *Hebrew* Tongue do all expound this Glorious Name of God ; they tell us, that this Glorious Name of his notes both his Being, and the Unchangeableneſs of his Being ; and when God, as in my Text, ſays, *I am Jehovah*, he does in one Word ſay, I am He, that Great He, who have my Being in and of my ſelf, and do give Being to all the Creatures, and who in my Being was from all Eternity, am now, and will
be

be one and the same for ever. The same thing does God assert of himself in that other Name of his, *Exod.* 3. 14. where he calls himself [*I am*,] *God said unto Moses, I am that I am; and he said, Thus shalt thou say unto the Children of* Israel, *I am hath sent me unto you.* I am what I am, or, I will what I will be, it notes Eternal and Unchangeable Being in himself, and that he is now, and will be for ever, that which he was before to *Abraham, Isaac* and *Jacob. It notes* (as a Learned Man observes) *the Necessity, Eternity, Immutability, and Infinite Fulness of God's Being, and indeed the Fountain of all Being to be in him.* It speaks him to be perpetually God, and to his Name Christ alludeth, when he asserts his own Divinity in *John* 8. 58. *Before* Abraham *was I am.* So *Psal.* 102. 27. *Thou art the same*, says the *Psalmist* to God, or, which is more suitable to the *Hebrew*, Thou art thy self, always thy self. Thus God is unchangeable in his Being or Essence; and when I say he is unchangeable in his Being or Essence, I say he is unchangeable in all his Essential Properties, his Wisdom, his Power, his Justice, his Holiness, his Omniscience, his All-sufficiency, and the like. For pray mark, The Attributes or Properties of God are not in him distinguisht either from his Essence, or from one another really, but notionally or virtually; that is, they are not distinguished at all in God, but are all one and the same Perfection in him; they are indeed, as was noted in the Beginning, the Divine Essence it self, according to that general Rule, whatever is in God is God, they are distinguished only in the manner of our Understanding, which being unable to comprehend that infinite pure Act at once, do conceive thereof after the manner of many Acts, so that I say, when we affirm that God is unchangeable in his Being or Essence, we affirm that he is unchangeable in all his Attributes and

and Perfections, in his Holiness, his Wisdom, his Power, his Greatness, his Love, and the like. I'll close this Head with a great Saying which I have read in *Austin, Thou* (says he to God) *alone art God, that Being which cannot possibly be changed either into a better or worse Being, because thou art a most simple Being;* to whom 'tis not one thing to live, and another thing to live blessedly, and that because thou art thine own Blessedness, of which more in the next Particular.

2. God is unchangeable in his Blessedness and Glory: The Lord *Jehovah* is a Glorious and Blessed God, *He is the Blessed,* as well as *the Only Potentate,* 1 *Tim.* 6. 15. He is Blessed, and that not only Objectively, as he is the great Object of the Praises, Blessings, and Admirings of Men and Angels for ever; nor yet as he is the Spring and Fountain of all that Blessedness which the one and the other of them do eternally enjoy; but Subjectively, being a God Infinitely Blessed and Happy: God is the most Happy and Blessed Being, he is so Blessed that 'tis more than all the Creatures, whether Men or Angels, can do to add the last Tittle or Jot to his Blessedness: Hence we read, That *their Goodness extendeth not to him,* Psal. 16. 2. And again, *Can a Man be profitable unto God? And is it gain to him that thou makest thy Ways perfect?* That is, 'Tis no Profit, no Gain to God, no Addition to his Happiness or Perfection, that we, or any, are or do so. See also *Job* 22. 2, 3. and *Chap.* 35. 7, 8. *If thou be righteous, what givest thou unto him? Or what receiveth he of thine Hand? Thy Wickedness may hurt a Man as thou art, and thy Righteousness may profit the Son of Man, but not God:* As if he should say, God is never the more Happy or Unhappy by any thing the Creature does or can do: 'Tis true, the Saints and Angels both do love him, praise him, admire and adore him for ever; they

call

be one and the fame for ever. The fame thing does God affert of himfelf in that other Name of his, *Exod.* 3. 14. where he calls himfelf [*I am*,] *God faid unto* Mofes, *I am that I am; and he faid, Thus fhalt thou fay unto the Children of* Ifrael, *I am hath fent me unto you.* I am what I am, or, I will what I will be, it notes Eternal and Unchangeable Being in himfelf, and that he is now, and will be for ever, that which he was before to *Abraham, I-faac* and *Jacob. It notes* (as a Learned Man ob-ferves) *the Neceffity, Eternity, Immutability, and Infinite Fulnefs of God's Being, and indeed the Fount ain of all Being to be in him.* It fpeaks him to be per-petually God, and to his Name Chrift alludeth, when he afferts his own Divinity in *John* 8. 58. *Before* Abraham *was I am.* So *Pfal.* 102. 27. *Thou art the fame,* fays the *Pfalmift* to God; or, which is more fuitable to the *Hebrew,* Thou art thy felf, always thy felf. Thus God is unchangeable in his Being or Effence; and when I fay he is unchange able in his Being or Effence, I fay he is unchange-able in all his Effential Properties, his Wifdom, his Power, his Juftice, his Holinefs, his Omnifci-ence, his All-fufficiency, and the like. For pray mark, The Attributes or Properties of God are not in him diftinguifht either from his Effence, or from one another really, but notionally or virtually; that is, they are not diftinguifhed at all in God, but are all one and the fame Perfection in him; they are in-deed, as was noted in the Beginning, the Divine Effence it felf, according to that general Rule, whatever is in God is God, they are diftinguifhed only in the manner of our Underftanding, which being unable to comprehend that infinite pure Act at once, do conceive thereof after the manner of many Acts, fo that I fay, when we affirm that God is unchangeable in his Being or Effence, we affirm that he is unchangeable in all his Attributes and

and Perfections, in his Holineſs, his Wiſdom, his Power, his Greatneſs, his Love, and the like. I'll cloſe this Head with a great Saying which I have read in *Auſtin, Thou* (ſays he to God) *alone art God, that Being which cannot poſſibly be changed either unto a better or worſe Being, becauſe thou art a moſt ſimple Being*; to whom 'tis not one thing to live, and another thing to live bleſſedly, and that becauſe thou art thine own Bleſſedneſs; of which more in the next Particular.

2. God is unchangeable in his Bleſſedneſs and Glory: The Lord *Jehovah* is a Glorious and Bleſſed God, *He is the Bleſſed*, as well as *the Only Potentate,* 1 *Tim.* 6. 15. He is Bleſſed, and that not only Objectively, as he is the great Object of the Praiſes, Bleſſings, and Admirings of Men and Angels for ever; nor yet as he is the Spring and Fountain of all that Bleſſedneſs which the one and the other of them do eternally enjoy; but Subjectively, being a God Infinitely Bleſſed and Happy: God is the moſt Happy and Bleſſed Being, he is ſo Bleſſed that 'tis more than all the Creatures, whether Men or Angels, can do to add the laſt Tittle or Iota to his Bleſſedneſs: Hence we read, That *their Goodneſs extendeth not to him,* Pſal. 16. 2. And again, *Can a Man be profitable unto God? And is it Gain to him that thou makeſt thy Ways perfect?* That is, 'Tis no Profit, no Gain to God, no Addition to his Happineſs or Perfection, that we, or any, are or do ſo. See alſo *Job* 22. 2, 3. and *Chap.* 35. , 8. *If thou be righteous, what giveſt thou unto him? Or what receiveth he of thine Hand? Thy Wickedneſs may hurt a Man as thou art, and thy Righteouſneſs may profit the Son of Man, but not God:* As if he ſhould ſay, God is never the more Happy or Unhappy by any thing the Creature does or can do: 'Tis true, the Saints and Angels both do love him, praiſe him, admire and adore him for ever; they

caſt

caft all their Crowns down at his Foot: But alas! this adds not one Jot to his Happiness; no, *He is exalted above all Blessing and Praise,* Nehem. 9. 5. Yea, 'tis a Stooping, a Condefcention in him to take Notice of thefe things, as you have it, *Pfal.* 113. 5, 6. And indeed, 'tis our Happinefs, not God's, to love him, ferve him, praife him, walk with him, and live to him. *Who art thou, Lord,* (fays *Aug.) and, what am I that thou fhouldeft command me to love thee, that thou wilt accept of Love from me, and threaten me with great Miferies unlefs I will love thee?* He admires the Condefcention of God herein. Yea, fuch is the Bleffednefs of God, that he himfelf cannot add hereunto, God cannot make himfelf more Bleffed, Happy and Perfect, than he is, nothing can by Infinitenefs be added unto Infinitenefs. Now as he is tnus Bleffed, fo his Bleffednefs is unchangeable, hence one of his Names is, *Over all, God Bleffed for evermore,* Rom. 9. 5. Ἐις τὸς αἰῶνας, throughout all Ages, and to all Eternity: Alas! God makes his People unchangeably Bleffed; and he that makes others unchangeably Bleffed, is doubtlefs unchangeable in his own Bleffednefs. But this will further appear by confidering a little what the Bleffednefs of God is, and wherein i does lye, it lyes wholly in that Infinite Delight, Solace and Satisfaction, which he hath in Himfelf, in the Vifion and Fruition of Himfelf, and thofe Infinite Glories and Perfections which are in him, and which he fees and knows will be in him for ever. (Firft,) God is an Infinite Ocean of Sweetnefs, Perfection, and Glory, he has all Good and all Perfection in him, as in its Fountain, Fulnefs, and Purity; as all the Lines in the Circumference do meet, and are united in the Center, fo all Excellencies and Perfections do meet and are united in God; and as God has all Excellencies and Perfections in him, fo (Secondly) he perfectly underftands his own Infinite Per

fefrom.

fections, contemplates them, and has an Infinite
Delight, Solace, and Satisfaction in them; he is
Infinitely Pleafed and at Reft in himfelf, ard in the
Vifion and Fruition of his own Perfections, and
this is his Bleffednefs; hence he tells us, that *he is
God All fufficient*, that is to fay, for and to himfelf,
as well as for and to his People, *Gen.* 17. 1. *I am
God All-fufficient*, I am my own Bleffednefs; and, *A-
braham*, I am thy Bleffednefs, and I have enough
for both. The Truth is, all our Happinefs lyes in
God, in the Knowledge and Enjoyment of God; *
This is Life eternal, to know thee the only true God,*
Joh. 17. 3. And *Happy is the People whofe God is
the Lord*, *Pfal.* 144. 15. *He that made me is
Good*, (fays *Auftin*) *and he is my Good, my Happinefs, and in him will I exult and rejoice above all my
other good things.* And 'tis a great Saying which he
has to the fame Purpofe elfewhere : *Unhappy
is that Man* (fays he) *who knows all other things,
but is ignorant of thee, O God; but bleffed is he who
knows thee, though he be ignorant of other things ; but
he that knows both thee and other things too, he is not
the more happy becaufe he knows other things, but he
is happy in thee only.* Thus our Happinefs lyes in
God and the Vifion of him; and where fhould
his own Happinefs lye but in himfelf ? He that is
the Spring and Fountain of our Happinefs, is an
everlafting Fountain of Happinefs to himfelf· *Thou
thy felf* (fays *Auftin*) *art thine own Happinefs.* I'll
clofe this Head with a great Saying of a Learned
Man , *God* (fays he) *is fuch an Infinitely Perfect and
Happy Being that nothing can be added to him, nothing
can be taken from him: He can want nothing out of
himfelf, nor can he receive any thing but from himfelf;
and he is Infinitely Sufficient for and to himfelf, having
all things in himfelf.*

3. God is unchangeable in his Counfels and De-
crees : We read in Scripture feveral times of the

Counfels of God ; *Thy Counfels of old are Faithfulnefs and Truth, Ifa. 25. 1.* And in *Eph.* 1. 11. he is faid *to work all things according to the Counfel of his own Will :* And the fame thing is elfewhere mentioned under the Notion, fometimes of his *Purpofe,* and fometimes his *Decree.* And to underfland this, you muft know that God from all Eternity did as it were fit in Council with his own Wifdom, Juftice, and Grace, and in that Council did abfolutely Decree and Determine the Futurition, that is to fay, the infallible future Being of whatever is befides himfelf, unto the Praife of his own Glory ; for that is the Purpofe, Counfel or Decree, of God ; 'tis his Free, Abfolute, and Eternal, Determining of all things which have been, are, or fhall be, fo as himfelf faw fitteft to have them, or, it is that one, free, conftant, Act of God, whereby he hath abfolutely determined all things in a Subferviency to his own Glory : Now in this Counfel or Decree of his he is unchangeable, and the fame for ever ; what he willeth he willeth always, his willing of things being one pure Act, without any Interruption or Shadow of Change, this the Scripture is full in *Pfal.* 33. 11. *The Counfel of the Lord ftandeth for ever, the Thoughts of his Heart to all Generations :* So *Prov.* 19. 21. *There are many Devices in a Man's Heart ; neverthelefs the Counfel of the Lord that fhall ftand.* Men may plot and fight againft God and his Counfel, but yet it will ftand, and that for ever : And you have this Truth afferted by God himfelf, you have it from his own Mouth, *Ifa.* 46. 10. *My Counfel fhall ftand* (fays God) *and I will do all my Pleafure.* God derides the Counfels of Men that oppofe him and his People, telling them exprefly that they fhall not ftand, *Ifa.* 8. 10. But as for his own Counfel that fhall ftand , hence alfo we read of the *Immutability of his Counfel,* Heb. 6. 17, 18. *God willing more abundantly*

dantly to shew unto the Heirs of Promise the Immuta-bility of his Counsel, confirmed it by an Oath, that by two immutable things, wherein it was impossible for God to lie, we might have strong Consolation, &c. Mark, *the Immutability of his Counsel,* and *Two Immutable Things, wherein it was impossible for God to lie:* That is, his Counsel and his Oath, and his Counsel confirmed by his Oath; confirmed, namely to our Faith, not in it self, for his Counsel in it self is as firm without as with his Oath, and his Oath is added meerly as an Indulgence and Condescention to our Weakness; therefore 'tis added, *that we might have strong Consolation*; and 'tis *to shew unto the Heirs of Promise,* &c. And as his Counsels in general, so his particular Counsels concerning Mens Eternal Estates are also immutable: *The Foundation of God standeth sure,* (says the Apostle) *having this Seal, the Lord knoweth who are his,* 2 *Tim.* 2. 19. By the Metaphor both of a Foundation and Seal. Here (as a Learned Man observes upon the Place) *is to be understood God's Decree of Election unto Eternal Life*; and this *standeth sure,* (says the Apostle) this changes, this varies not, and to the same Purpose *Calvin* speaks upon the Place. *The Apostle,* (says he) *calls us to look back upon the Election of God, which he stiles a Foundation, hereby shewing the firm and stable Constancy or Immutability of it.* So *Rom.* 9. 11. *That the Purpose of God according to Election might stand.* God will have his own Eternal Purpose according to his Election stand, and stand it shall, and that for ever. Thus God is unchangeable in his Counsels: Alas! all his Counsels are Free, Wise, Absolute, Powerful, Counsels, and therefore they cannot change: And this *Calvin* takes to be a special part of the Meaning of the Text; namely, God's Unchangeableness in his Counsels; for thus he speaks. *God* (says he) *remains firm and stedfast in his own Purposes, nor*

B *is*

is he bended or varied this way and that way, as *Men* oftentimes repent of, and change their own *Counsels*, because things come into their *Mind* which they thought not of before, and so they wish that undone which they have done, and do seek ways of retracting their own *Acts*, and 'tis a Saying I have read in *Austin*; God (says he) changes his *Works*, not his *Counsels*. O let us reverence and adore God in this his Unchangeableness!

4. God is unchangeable in his Kingdom and Rule · God has a Kingdom and Dominion over the whole Wor'd, which Kingdom and Dominion of his is that Absolute Right and Power whereby he possesseth all things as his own, and also orders and disposes of them as he pleases, ruling and governing the whole World according to the Counsel of his own Will, and in a Subserviency to his own most Wise and Holy Ends; hence he is said *to be over all, Rom.* 9. 5. and *above all, Eph.* 4. 6. to wit, in Kingdom, Power, and Dominion, he has a Right to all, and he has the Ordering and Dispose of all, both Persons and Things, States and Kingdoms: *He is the most High that ruleth in the Kingdoms of Men, and gives them to whomsoever he will,* Dan. 4. 32. He works all, and orders all, in the Kingdom of Providence, as well as in the Kingdom of Grace, and that *according to the Counsel of his own Will, Eph.* 1. 11. He rules and commands all, *He hath prepared his Throne in the Heavens, and his Kingdom ruleth over all,* Psal. 103 19. *He doth whatsoever he pleases in Heaven and on Earth, in the Seas, and in all deep Places,* Psal. 135. 6. Now in this Kingdom and Dominion of his he is Unchangeable; it admits of neither Stop nor Period, he ruleth by his Power for ever, Psal. 66. 7. *Thy Kingdom, O Lord, is an everlasting Kingdom, a Kingdom of Ages, and thy Dominion endureth throughout all Generations,* Psal. 145. 13. *And I blessed the most High,*

High, (ſays *Nebuchadnezzar*) *whoſe Dominion is an everlaſting Dominion, and his Kingdom from Generation to Generation, Dan.* 4. 34. Ah, Sirs, whatever Men think, yet God governs the World, and his Dominion is over all; *The Lord reigns,* (ſaith the *Pſalmiſt*) *Pſal.* 93. 1. He hath reigned, he doth reign, and he will reign for ever: There is a Day coming when *all Rule, Authority and Power, ſhall be put down,* and that once for all, even the Principality of the Angels themſelves (as *Calvin* obſerves) not excepted, 1 *Cor.* 15. 24. But God reigns for ever and ever, and his Kingdom has no End: Thus he is unchangeable in his Kingdom and Rule in the World, which is a great Encouragement to the People of God: O my Beloved, God governs the World now as well as heretofore; yea, and he governs it in our Nature now as well as heretofore, *John* 5. 27. He governs all by the Man Chriſt, who has a natural tender Care of, and Reſpe& to, his Church and People in all, let us therefore ſay with the *Pſalmiſt, The Lord reigneth, let the People tremble, the Lord reigneth, let Sion rejoice:* God is not, God cannot be, put by his Throne and Kingdom.

5. God is unchangeable in his Covenant and Promiſe, his Covenant and Promiſe with his People in Chriſt: God hath made a Covenant with his People in Chriſt, a Covenant of Peace, a Covenant of Grace, a Covenant of Love, a Covenant founded upon Grace, a Covenant full of Grace, a Covenant wholly made up of Grace and Love, from firſt to laſt, therefore called *Grace* in the Abſtract, *Rom.* 6. 14. a Full Covenant, a Rich Covenant, a Precious Covenant, a Covenant made up of Rich, yea, exceeding Rich and, Precious, Promiſes, and filled with exceeding Rich and Precious Treaſures, precious *Grace,* precious *Peace,* precious *Pardon,* precious *Righteouſneſs,* precious *Salvation;* with a

precious

precious *God*, a precious *Chrift*, a precious *Spirit*,
a precious *Heaven* and *Bleſſedneſs* for ever   Now
in this Covenant, and in all the precious Promiſes
of it, is God the Lord unchangeable : Hence you
have it ſo often called *an Everlaſting Covenant* , *I
will eſtabliſh my Covenant between me and thee* (ſays
God to *Abraham*) *for an Everlaſting Covenant, to
be a God unto thee, and to thy Seed after thee*, Gen.
17. 7. Again, *I will make an Everlaſting Covenant
with them* (ſpeaking of his People) *and I will not
turn away from them to do them good*, Jer. 32. 40.
and as an Everlaſting Covenant, ſo an *Everlaſting
and Sure Covenant* ; *God hath made with me an Everlaſting Covenant*, (ſays *David*) *well ordered in all
things, and ſure*, 2 Sam. 23. 5.   And again, *Come,
and I will make with you an Everlaſting Covenant,
even the ſure Mercies of* David, *Iſa.* 55. 3.   Hence
alſo 'tis called a *Covenant of Salt*, Num. 18. 19.
that is, a firm, a durable, an unchangeable, Covenant.
Many other Ways does God ſet forth the Immutability of his Covenant, and that for the Encouragement of our Faith and Comfort. How ſweet
is that .Word, and what a Reſt may it be to Faith?
Iſa. 54. 9, 10. *This is as the Waters of* Noah *unto me;
for as I have ſworn that the Waters of* Noah *ſhould no
more go over the Earth, ſo have I ſworn that I will no
more be wroth with thee, nor rebuke thee : For the
Mountains ſhall depart, and the Hills be removed, but
my Kindneſs ſhall not depart from thee, neither ſhall
the Covenant of my Peace be removed, ſaith the Lord,
that hath Mercy on thee.* Pray obſerve, God had in
the two foregoing Verſes promiſed his Church and
People, that, *though for a ſmall Moment he had for-
ſaken them, yet with great Mercies he would gather
them; and that though in a little Wroth he had hid his
Face from them for a Moment, yet with Everlaſting
Kindneſs he would have Mercy on them :* And here
in theſe two Verſes he gives them a double Ground
of

of the Aſſurance hereof; the one taken from his Oath, and the Unchangeableneſs thereof, *Verſ. 9.* the other from his Covenant, and the Unchangeableneſs thereof, *Ver. 10. For the Mountains ſhall depart,* &c. as if he ſhould ſay, The Mountains and Hills may ſooner be removed than my Covenant; yea, the time will come when theſe ſhall be removed, but the time will never come that my Covenant ſhall fail or be removed. But what if his People ſin, what then ? Why then he will correct and chaſtiſe them for their Sin, but his Covenant he will keep firm and inviolable for ever notwithſtanding· For this you have a full and an expreſs Text, *Pſal.* 89. 30, 31, 32, 33, 34. *If his Children forſake my Law, and walk not in my Judgments; if they break my Statutes, and keep not my Commandments; then will I viſit their Tranſgreſſions with a Rod, and their Iniquities with Stripes. Nevertheleſs (O Gracious* Nevertheleſs*) my Loving kindneſs will I not take from him, nor ſuffer my Faithfulneſs to fail, my Covenant will I not break,* &c. We ſin and break, and break and ſin, and God chaſtiſes us, it may be, for our Sin, but yet ſtill his Covenant remains firm and unchangeable. So 2 *Tim.* 2. 13. *If we believe not, yet he abideth faithful, he cannot deny himſelf·* Oh, I have an unbelieving Heart, and I ſhall, I fear, forfeit all ; although thou haſt an unbelieving Heart, yet God remains faithful. Thus God is unchangeable in his Covenant ; alas ! his Covenant is built upon unchangeable Love, and ſealed with unchangeable Blood, and cannot therefore but be unchangeable: And, as the Covenant, ſo all the Promiſes of the Covenant, are ſure and unchangeable, *they are all Yea and Amen in Chriſt,* 2 *Cor.* 1. 20. that is, they are all ſure, firm, unchangeable, Promiſes, Promiſes that will certainly be made good . Men promiſe many times, and change, but God promiſes, and changes not ; and

this

this some conceive to be held forth in that Name of his, *I am*, Exod. 3. 14. *I am that I am*, or, I am what I was, or, I will be what I was; that is, as one expounds it, *I will be in my Performances, what I was in my Promises:* God makes good all his Promises to a Tittle. He that is Truth it self, and Faithfulness it self, cannot lie, cannot fail. 'Tis a sweet Saying I have read in *Austin*, *They are thy Promises, O Lord, and who need fear being deserved when Truth it self promises?* Oh, we need not fear, we need not question, for God is true, God is faithful; Oh, how sweet are the Thoughts of an unchangeable Covenant, God has laid himself under Bonds to his People, when he was infinitely free in himself, and under Bonds to do great things for them, to pardon their Iniquities, Transgressions and Sins; to give them a new Heart and a new Spirit, to pour out his Spirit upon them, to cause them to walk in his Statutes and Judgments to do them, to write his Laws in their Hearts, and put them into their inward Parts, to cleanse them from all their Filthiness and Idols, to put his Fear into their Hearts that they shall never depart from him, and (which is all in one) to be a God unto them, and that they shall be his People, that is, he has laid himself under Bonds to be to them, and to do for them, what a God can be to and do for them, and he is firm and unchangeable in all, and all shall assuredly have its Accomplishment in its Season. Oh, how sweet is this? This was *David*'s Death-bed Cordial, 2 *Sam* 23 5. *Although my House be not so with God, yet he hath made with me an Everlasting Covenant, and this is all my Salvation and all my Desire*, and indeed well it might, for what could *David* or any desire more than is contained in God's Covenant, which has Heaven on Earth, God and the Creature, Time and Eternity, all in it? Oh, study this Covenant

o

of God, and the Unchangeablenefs of it, and you
will find it an unchangeable Spring of Comfort to
you. God himfelf found Fault with the firft Covenant, 'tis faid, and why ? Wny, becaufe it
made no Provifion for his People againft Sin, but
you will be able to find no Fault with this Cove
nant, this being *well ordered in all things, and fure ;*
as in the Place laft quoted you have it.

6. God is unchangeable in his Grace and Love
to his People. God loves his People, and that
with a Choice and peculiar Love, a Love like that
wherewith he loves Chrift himfelf, *Joh.* 17. 23.
They are indeed *the Dearly Beloved of his Soul,* as
you have it, *Jer.* 12. 7. and in this Love of his
towards them he is unchangeable, always the fame,
which I fhall at once a little open and evince unto
you in Three Propofitions.

1. God is unchangeable in his Love it felf to his
People, that being always the fame towards them;
I have loved thee (fays God to his People) *with an
Everlafting Love, Jer* 31. 3. with a Love that is
from Everlafting to Everlafting, without Change
or Period, God's Love to his People is fo firm and
ftable that nothing whatever can poffibly null or
alter it, nothing can poffibly caft them out of his
Heart, if any thing could do it, it would be their
Sinnings againft him, and their Breakings with
him, but thefe do not, cannot, do it, fo he has
told us, *Pfal.* 89. 30, 31, 32, 33. If they fin, I'll
correct them for their Sin, *but my Loving-kindnefs
I will not take from them ;* (or, as fome render it,)
I will not fo much as interrupt my Love towards
them ; as if he fhould fay, though they fin, yet
I'd love them ftill God does not love the Sins of
his People, no, he hates them, but he loves their
Perfons notwithftanding their Sins But when if
Afflictions and Temptations be added to their Sins,
and both the one and the other rife high, will no

this

this break off his Love from them ? No, see that
Triumph of the *Apostle* upon this Account, *Rom.* 8.
ult. *Who shall separate us from the Love of God ? Shall
Tribulation, or Distress, or Persecution, and the like ?
Nay, in all these things we are more than Conquerors,
through him that loved us , for I am perswaded that
neither Death, nor Life, nor Angels, nor Principalities,
nor Powers, nor Things present, nor Things to come, nor
Height, nor Depth, nor any other Creature, shall be able
to separate us from the Love of God which is in Christ
Jesus our Lord.* Here you see are Afflictions and
Temptations added to Sins , yea, here are Heights
and Depths of these things, but all cannot separate
God's People from his Love, nor cast them out of
his Heart. One I remember gives the Sum of the
whole in this short Word ; *God hath loved from E-
ternity, and he will love to Eternity.* The Truth is,
could either Sins or Sufferings cast us out of God's
Heart, and separate us from his Love, who then
among the Saints could hope to continue in his
Love, and upon his Heart ? Besides, in the Place
lately quoted, *Isa.* 54. 9, 10. God says expresly,
that though the Mountains should be removed , yet
his Kindness to his People should not be removed ,
no, that remains firm and stedfast for ever. True,
God may possibly afflict his People, and that many
ways, and very sorely ; he may speak against them
as against *Ephraim, Jer.* 31. 20. write against them,
and that bitter things, as against *Job, Job* 13. 26.
He may fight against them, as against those, *Isa.*
63. 10. He may frown upon them, and let in his
Terrors into them, as he did upon and into *He-
man, Psal.* 88. ult. But yet still he loves them,
still they are dear to him.

2. God is unchangeable in all the special saving
Fruits and Effects of his Love to his People, *Rom.*
11. 29. *The Gifts and Calling of God are without Repentance ;* that is, the Gifts of his effectual Calling,

or his faving Gifts, such as effectual Calling, and
the like, fhall never be repented of, never be re-
called or reverfed by him, as they who receive
thofe Gifts will have no Caufe to repent, but to
rejoice in them for ever, fo God who gives them,
will not repent that he gave them to them. God
gives Chrift, he gives Grace, he gives Peace, he
gives Pardon, he gives Righteoufnefs, he gives Salvation, he gives Eternal Life to his People, and
all out of his Love to them; and he never recalls or
reverfes thefe Fruits and Effects of Love. You
have another full Text for this, *Jam.* 1. 17. *Every
good and every perfect Gift is from above, and cometh
down from the Father of Lights, with whom is no variablenefs, nor Shadow of turning.* Mark, Having
fpoken of the perfect Gifts of God, prefently he
adds, *with whom is no Variablenefs*, as if he fhould
fay, as all good and faving Gifts come from God,
fo he is unchangeable in all. Indeed there are
common Gifts, and Gifts of a meer outward Calling, which God out of a common Love and Boun-
ty gives to Men, and thefe many times he recalls,
they not improving them : So the Talent was taken
from the flothful Servant, *Mat* 25. 28. and you
know what Chrift fpeaks immediately thereupon,
v. 29. *Unto every one that hath fhall be given, and
he fhall have Abundance, but from him that hath
not, fhall be taken away even that which he hath.*
Pray obferve, *To him that hath fhall be given,* that
is, whoever God hath beftowed Gifts and Talents
upon, and he improves them for God and his own
Salvation, he fhall have more Gifts and more Talents, he fhall have an abundant Increafe of thefe
things. *But from him that hath not, fhall be taken
away even that which he hath.* Here feems to be a
Contradiction, *Him that hath not,* and yet *what he
has,* the Meaning in fhort is this That when
God beftows fuch and fuch Gifts and Talents upon

a Perfon to be employed for his Glory, and he
does not fo employ them, he does not rightly ufe
and improve them, what God hath beftowed upon
him fhall be taken away: But 'tis otherwife with
the faving Gifts and Fruits of God's fpecial Love,
thefe God never rever recalls, which is a fweet
Contemplation. Soul! hath God beftowed fome
of his faving Gifts upon thee? Then they are thine
for ever: Has he given thee his Chrift? He will
never repent of it, never call him back again, but
fweet Jefus is thine for ever· Has he given thee
his Spirit? He will never repent of it, nor will he
ever recall this Bleffed Gift from thee, the Holy,
Good, and Glorious, Spirit is thine for ever. Has
he given thee a New and Spiritual Life? Has he
given thee Grace, Pardon, Righteoufnefs, Jufti-
fication, and the like? He will never repent of it,
all thefe are thine for ever O how fweet is this
to contemplate! Thou may'ft fit down and fay,
Chrift is mine, the Comforter is mine, Life, Peace,
Pardon, Righteoufnefs, Salvation, are all mine,
and that for ever.

3. God is unchangeable in the real Defigns and
Workings of his Love. I fay, real, though not
fenfible, God's Love to his People may be fufpend-
ed and interrupted as to the fenfible Influences and
Manifeftations thereof, but yet even then 'tis
active and really at Work for them, however the
outward Difpenfation may vary, now fmile, then
frown, now lift up, then caft down, now fill,
then empty; now form Light, then create Darknefs, yet in all ftill he goes on in one even conftant Tenure of Love towards them, in all his
Love is at Work for them, and towards them, and
he intends and defigns them as much Love in one
as in the other, and accordingly firft or laft effects
and accomplishes it And this is but agreeable to
his Covenant with them, and Promife to them, *Jo.*
3 2.

32. 40. *I'll make* (fays he to his People) *an Everlasting Covenant with you, never to turn away from you to do you good.* And, *All things shall work together for Good to them that love God, Rom.* 8. 28. Whatever God does with us, however he feems to carry it towards us, yet still he is doing us good, and acting his Love towards us, *We* (as an Holy Man fpeaks) *are apt to think that God shews us Love when he doth some great thing for us, but* (faith he) *God is always acting out his Love towards us when he frowns, as well as when he smiles; when he withdraws, as well as when he approaches to us.* In a Word, Soul! whatever God does there is Love in it, and he defigns thee Love and Good by it. Does he fmile, give, fill, keep alive, draw near to thee? In all there is Love, his fpecial Love works and runs through all, or, does he frown, take, empty, kill, hide his Face? In all this there is Love, yea, the fame fpecial Love of his works in all, and runs through all; God is acting out his Love to thee in the one as well as the other. O how fweet is this! Death to the People of God comes from the fame Fountain of Love in God's Heart that Life does.

CHAP.

CHAP. IV.

Which gives an Account why or whence it is that God is Unchangeable.

THat God is unchangeable, as also wherein, you have already seen. That which falls next under Consideration, is to shew whence it is that God is indeed thus unchangeable ; or if you will, what Basis and Foundation the Unchangeableness of God is built upon : 'Tis built upon a Threefold Basis or Foundation:

1. The Infinite Purity and Simplicity of his Nature.
2. The Infinite Excellency and Perfection of his Being.
3. The Infinite Extent and Compass of his Wisdom.

1. The Unchangeableness of God is built upon, or springs from, the Infinite Purity and Simplicity of his Nature. God, my Beloved, is a most pure Act, he is a *Spirit*, an Infinite Spirit, *Joh.* 4. 24. and so an infinitely pure, simple, uncompounded, Being, and therefore unchangeable. *God* (says a Learned Man) *is a most simply and perfectly pure Act, free from all Composition ; and therefore cannot possibly be dissolved, corrupted, or wax old and decay.* And *Austin*, I remember, founds God's Unchangeableness upon this Ground or Basis · *Thou only art God,* (says he) *and canst not be changed, either into a better or worse Being than what thou art, because thou art a most pure and simple Being.* Men, and so other Creatures, have their Mixtures and Compositions, they are compounded and made up of
different

different Elements, Qualities and Humours, and that is one Reaſon among others why they change; but God is a moſt pure ſimple Being, he is Purity and Simplicity it ſelf, and therefore unchangeable. Angels and Souls have a Compoſition in them, they are compounded of Subject and Accidents, Nature and Qualities, or Graces, but God is one meer and perfect Act, without all Compoſition, Diviſion, Multiplication, or the like, and therefore without Change. Where there is Compoſition, there may be Mutation; but where there is infinite Simplicity, there is abſolute Immutability, and thus 'tis you ſee with God.

2. The Unchangeableneſs of God is built upon, and ariſes, from the Infinite Excellency and Perfection of his Being. As God is a moſt pure and ſimple, ſo he is a moſt perfect, Being, an infinitely perfect Being, and therefore unchangeable : Men are imperfect, and therefore they change; God is perfect, and therefore he changes not. All Change, my Beloved, argues Imperfection in the Subject changed. For, pray obſerve, there is a twofold Change, there is a Corruptive, and there is a Perfective, Change, a Corruptive Change is a Change from good to bad, or from bad to worſe, and ſuch a Change to be ſure argues Imperfection in the Subject, a Perfective Change is a Change from bad to good, or from good to better, and this alſo argues Imperfection in the Subject; this argues the Subject to be imperfect before, whatever 't s now : Thus all Change neceſſarily argues Imperfection; but God is infinitely perfect, and therefore not ſubject to Change; he is capable of no Corruptive, nor yet a Perfective, Change, becauſe he is an infinitely perfect Being, and ſo can have nothing added to him, nothing taken from him. *Be ye perfect* (ſays Chriſt) *as your Heavenly Father is perfect, Mat.* 5, 48. Our Heavenly Father

ther is a perfect Being, he is both essentially and
originally perfect, he is perfect in himself, ha-
ing all Excellencies and Perfections centring in
him; and he is the Spring and Cause of all those
Excellencies and Perfections that are found in the
Creatures: *God is Light*, (says St. *John*) *and in
him is no Darkness at all*, 1 *Joh.* 1. 5. that is, he is
both pure and perfect, pure without Mixture, and
perfect without Defect, he is wholly Perfection,
and therefore unchangeable. What shall I say?
God is so good, so full, so blessed, so every way
perfect, that 'tis impossible he should change. 'Tis
a great Speech I have read in one of the Ancients,
*For thee, or to thee, Lord, to be and to live, are not
two things, because thou art the chief Being, and the
chief Life; thou art every way the Highest, the Chief-
est, the most Excellent, and thou art not changed.*
And indeed therefore he cannot change. My Beloved, God has told us, that he is God All-sufficient, *I am God All-mighty*, (says he) or *God All-sufficient*, I have all Fulness, Blessedness, and Perfection, in me *He* (as one upon the Place notes)
*is most sufficient, one who is infinitely sufficient for
himself, and who also vouchsafes a Sufficiency to his
People.* He has all Excellency and Perfection in
him, and that in a blessed Union and Conjunction,
and how then should he change?

3. The Unchangeableness of God is built upon,
and springs from, the infinite Fulness and Extent
of his Wisdom and Understanding: As God is a
most pure and perfect, so he is a most wise, Being,
and therefore unchangeable, and this referrs prin-
cipally to his Unchangeableness in his Kingdom,
Counsels, Covenant and Love. Mens Wisdom is
weak, and their Understandings dark and shallow,
and therefore they Change, they are not to Day
what they were Yesterday, nor will they be to
Morrow perhaps what they are to Day, but God

is infinitely wiſe, and knows all things, and there-fore he changes not; he is the ſame for ever. *Men change,* (ſays *Calvin*) *they oftentimes wiſh the things undone, which they have done, and ſeek Ways of retracting their own Acts or Grants, becauſe with them things come to mind many times which they fore-ſaw not, nor ever thought of :* But (ſays he) *God de-nies any ſuch thing to be found with him* , *he is infi-nitely wiſe, he has a perfect Knowledge and Under-ſtanding of things, and therefore changes not :* He is called in Scripture *a God of Knowledge,* 1 *Sam.* 2. 3. Yea, he is ſaid to be *perfect in Knowledge,* *Job* 37. 16. he has a perfect Knowledge of all things, whe-ther paſt, preſent, or to come , he ſees and knows all things at once, *uno intuitu,* with one Proſpect, or by one ſingle Aſpect, and that unerr-ingly and infallibly . He knows all things by one moſt ſimple, immutable, and eternal, Act of Un-derſtanding; God is in Scripture ſtiled *the only wiſe God,* 1 *Tim.* 1. 17. and *his Underſtanding is* ſaid to be *infinite, Pſal.* 147. 5. God, my Be-loved, ſees and knows himſelf, and in himſelf, all things, always, perfectly, and at once, all things without Exception , always without Inter-ruption , perfectly without Defect , and at once without Succeſſion , *Known unto God are all his Works from the Foundation of the World,* (ſays the A-poſtle) *Acts* 15. 18. In a Word, my Beloved, God has a perfect Proſpect of all things in his E-ternity, neither can there be any thing new to him, that ſhould occaſion a Change in him And thus you ſee upon what Baſis or Foundation the Unchangeableneſs of God is built.

C H A P.

CHAP. V.

*Several Propositions laid down for the ob-
viating of Objections, and the vindi-
cating of God's Unchangeableness from
all Cavil and Contradiction.*

THE next Work we have to do, is to vindicate the Unchangeableness of God from all
Cavils and Contradiction, and to obviate such Objections as may seem to lye against it, which I shall
do by making good these Four Propositions.

1. The First Proposition is this; That God's
repenting, which we sometimes read of in Scripture, is no way inconfiftent with, or repugnant
to the Truth and Glory of his Unchangeableness.
Oftentimes in Scripture God is said to repent, and
he is said to repent both of what he has done, and
also of what he hath said he would do. First, He
is said to repent of some things he had done. So
he is said *to repent that ever he made Man,* Gen. 6.
6. *It repented the Lord that he had made Man on the
Earth, and it grieved him at his Heart.* So it repented him that he had made Saul King, 1 Sam. 15.
11. *It repenteth me* (says God) *that I have set up
Saul to be King.* Secondly, God is said to repent
of some things which he hath said he would do.
So, *Pfal.* 135. 14. *The Lord will repent him concerning his Servants.* So, *Jer.* 26. 19. *The Lord repented him of the Evil which he had pronounced against
them,* with many other Places which might be
mentioned. Thus God is said to repent both ways.
Now Repentance imports a Change, and how
then is God unchangeable? I Answer, Never the
less unchangeable because of his repenting, for,
pray

pray obferve, when God is faid in Scripture to repent, 'tis to be *underftood* not in a proper, but in
an improper and allufive, Senfe , not *affective*, but
effective ; not according to his internal Will, but
an external Work . God is therefore faid to repent,
becaufe he doth as Men do when they repent, that
is, he changeth his Deeds, yet without any Change
of his Will ; yea, the Change of his Deeds is the
Execution of his unchangeable Will . When Men
repent, they ceafe to do what they had begun, and
they are ready to deftroy what they had wrought,,
and thus God is faid to repent, not becaufe his
Mind is changed, but becaufe he ceafeth to do
what he did, or he deftroyeth what he had made :
Thus he is faid *to repent of his making* Saul *King*, becaufe he meant to remove him from being King ;
and *to repent of his making Man*, becaufe he meant
to deftroy Man for his Sin. Now fuch repenting
does not argue the leaft Change in God, and therefore in the very fame Place where he is faid thus
to repent, he is alfo faid not to repent, as 1 *Sam.*
15. 11. & 29. 11. he is faid *to repent of making*
Saul *King :* And in *verf.* 29. 'tis faid of him, *that*
he will not lie, nor repent, nor is he a Man that he
fhould repent; he can no more repent in a proper
Senfe, as Repentance imports Change, than he
can lie ; and when, as there 'tis faid of him, that
he is not a Man that he fhould repent, there is thus
much implied, That he muft ceafe to be God, and
become Man, if he fo repents as to note Change
in him. 'Tis a good, and indeed a great, Obfer-
vation which one has upon this Place , *No Repen-*
tance (fays he) *can properly befal God, whereas he is*
Immutable, moft Wife, moft Bleffed, but he is faid to
repent, when he retracts and revokes his Benefits from
a Perfon or People. In a Word, he is faid to repent, *quoad effectorum mutationem*, as to the Change
of Effects, but *non quoad feipfum*, not as to himfelf,

in

in either his Nature or Will: But this will appear
further in the next Propofition. Therefore,

2. The Second Propofition is this, That the Non-
execution and Accomplifhment of fome Threats
and Promifes of God, which we find in his Word,
is no Impeachment of his Unchangeablenefs.
True, there are many things both threatned and
promifed by God in his Word that do never come
to pafs, God fometimes threatens what he does not
execute, as in the Cafe of *Hezekiah,* 2 *Kings* 20.
1, and 5. compared, and of *Nineveh, Jon.* 3. 4.
with 10. On the other Hand, God fometimes promifes that which is never accomplifhed, of which
Inftances not a few might be given. Now does
not this impeach and contradict his unchangeablenefs ? I Anfwer, No ; neither the one nor the
other of thefe is any way repugnant or contradi-
ctory thereunto : For, pray confider, thofe
Threatnings and Promifes which are not accomplifh'd, are not abfolute, but conditional, Threatnings and Promifes, Threatnings and Promifes
that have either an exprefs or implicit Condition
in them, which Condition being wanting, the
Non-accomplifhment of the Threat or Promife is
fo far from being inconfiftent with, that it ftrong-
ly argues the unchangeablenefs of God. I fhall
illuftrate this by fome Inftances, *Jer.* 18. 7, 8, 9, 10.
*At what inftant I fhall fpeak concerning a Nation, and
concerning a Kingdom, to pluck up, and to pull down,
and to deftroy it, if that Nation, againft whom I
have pronounced, turn from their Evil, I will repent
of the Evil that I thought to do unto them And at
what inftant I fhall fpeak concerning a Nation, and
concerning a Kingdom, to build and to plant it, if it
do evil in my Sight, that it obey not my Voice, then I
will repent of the Good wherewith I faid I would bene-
fit them.* Mark, here is both Evil threatned, and
Good promifed, but both under a Condition,

now,

now, if the Condition, upon which the one is threatned, and the other is promifed, be wanting, let it not be imputed to any Change in God, if either the one or the other be not accomplifh'd. When an Evil is threatned, and not executed, and when a Good is promifed, and not performed, the Non-execution of the one, and the Non-performance of the other, is not becaufe God is not unchangeable, but becaufe the Condition upon which the one was threatned, and the other promifed, is found wanting. I might argue in like manner from *Pfal.* 7. 12. *Luke* 13. *begin. Rev.* 2. 22. But let this one fuffice inftead of all the reft. And to this Purpofe fpeaks a Learned Man. *God* (fays he) *changes his Sentence,* the outward Threatning or Promife, *but not his Decree,* not his inward Counfel or Purpofe. And to the fame Effect is the Saying of another ; *If* (fays he) *we refpect the Counfel of God, that he does not, he cannot, change, but his Mind and Will revealed by the Prophets that is often changed.* And 'tis a great Saying of one of the School-men, *'Tis one thing* (fays he) *for God to change his Will, and another thing to will a Change*. God often wills and determines a Change, but he never changes his Will or Determination, thus where an Evil is threatned, or a Good promifed, which is not accomplifh'd, the Non-accomplifhment of it is not becaufe God is not unchangeable, but becaufe the Threat or Promife was conditional, and the Condition thereof was wanting.

3. The Third Propofition is this, That none of thofe Changes, which feem to be attributed to God in Scripture, are really oppofite to his unchangeablenefs. I grant, the Scripture feveral times reprefents God, feemingly at leaft, under Changes to us; fometimes he is reprefented as being changed from an Enemy to a Friend, to be
reconciled

reconciled to them with whom he was offended before, hence we read of his *being pacified towards Sinners, Ezek. 16. 63.* So *Isa* 12. 1. *Though thou waft angry with me,* (says the Church to God) *yet thine Anger is turned away.* Again, sometimes God is represented as being changed from a Friend to an Enemy, to be at War with them with whom he was before at Peace. So *Job* 30. 21. *Thou art become cruel to me* ; or, thou art turned or changed, *q. d.* Thou wert good and gracious, but now thou art severe and cruel. So *Isa.* 63. 10. *He was turned to be their Enemy, and fought against them.* Thus both these Ways God seems to be represented under Changes; and how then is he unchangeable? Nevertheless unchangeable for all this, and to vindicate God's Unchangeableness notwithstanding this, I wou'd intreat you to confider Two Things.

1. Confider, that God is unchangeable under the moft various and changeable Difpenfations that he does or can walk in towards us. 'Tis true, the external Difpenfation changes, his outward Courfe and Carriage towards us is very changeable and various, now he fmiles, and then he frowns, now he fills, and then he empties, now he lifts, and then he cafts down, now he breaks, and then he binds up, &c. Thus the outward Dealings and Difpenfations of God are very changeable and various; yet in and under all he himself changes not, but is ftill the fame, the fame in his Being and in his Bleffednefs, and the fame in his Counfel, Covenant, and Love to us. Hence, *Pfal.* 25. 10. *All the Paths* (that is, the Providences and Difpenfations) *of the Lord are* faid to be *Mercy and Truth to his People :* His Paths towards them are very various in themfelves, but God's Love and Grace is the fame in all. The outward Difpenfation of God toward us, it may be, is changed, he
did

did fmile, but now he frowns; he did give, but
now he takes away , he did form Light, but now
he creates Darknefs for us ; and hereupon we apprehend that God Himfelf, his Heart, his Counfel,
his Covenant, his Love, is changed , but 'tis only
in our Apprehenfion; for Indeed, and in Truth,
he is the fame ftill; the moft variable of his Difpenfations do not argue the leaft Variablenefs in
him at all; and indeed, where he is a Friend, he
is a Friend for ever, and where he is an Enemy,
he is an Enemy for ever, the Change is only in
the external Difpenfation.

2. Confider, that the Change is in us, and not
in God ; God is always the fame, but we are not
the fame; when God is pacified towards thofe
with whom he was offended, they are changed,
not he, he is the fame he was; and when he is
angry with Saints, with whom he was before at
Peace, they are changed, not he: The Change
was in *Job*, not in God, when he faid, *Thou art
turned to be cruel to me*: The Change was in the
Church, not in God, when he was faid to be
turned to be their Enemy. God (fays a Worthy Divine) *is the fame, his Love is the fame, his Wrath
is the fame, his Mercy is the fame, his Juftice is the
fame, and that for ever ; but we changing are caft
fometimes under the Effects of his Love, and fometimes under the Effects of his Wrath; we are fometimes under the faddeft Droppings of his Juftice, and
fometimes under the fweeteft Influences of his Mercy.*
As a Man that changes his Afpect, and turns about
his Body to another Point of the Heavens, that
Part of the Heavens which was before at his Right
Hand, is now at his Left. Not but that the Heavens are as they were, they change not, either
their Pofition or Motion, but the Man hath changed
his. So the Wrath and Love, the Juftice and
Mercy, of God ftand always at the fame Point, but

we

we turn, fometimes Juftice-ward, fometimes Mer
cy-ward ; now we face his Wrath, and then his
Love ; thus the Change is in us, and not in God,
and fo he remains unchangeable ftill.

4. The Fourth Propofition is this, That God's
Unchangeablenefs does no way exclude or invalidate the Ufe of Means . If God be unchangeable,
then to what Purpofe is the Ufe of Means ? Why
do we pray, or hear, or ufe, any Means in order
to our eternal Good ? Why, my Beloved, God's
Unchangeablenefs does no way exclude or invalidate the Ufe of Means, for pray confider, (Firft)
That God wills the Means as well as the End, and
the Means in order to the End , he wills our Praying as well as our Pardon, our Hearing as well as
our Happinefs, our Sowing as well as our Reaping,
our Sowing in the Ufe of Means as well as our
Reaping in the Harveft of Mercy. He wills our
Believing as our Bleffednefs, he wills the one as
well as the other ; yea, he wills the one in order
to the other, and that with the fame abfolute immutable and eternal Will ; *He hath ordained we*
fhould walk in good Works, Eph. 2. 10. and *he hath*
chofen us to Salvation, through the Sanctification of the
Spirit, and the Belief of the Truth, 2 Thef. 2. 13.
(Secondly) Confider, that as God wills the Means
as well as the End, fo through the Ufe of thefe it
it, that he gives out himfelf and his Bleffings to us,
and at laft brings us to the End : God makes a
Covenant with his People, and therein lays himfelf under Bonds to do great things for them, as
great as a God can do ; but he will have them pray
for them, nor will he do them but in a Way of
Prayer, Ezek. 36. 37. and God tells us, that *he ne-*
ver faid to 'the Seed of Jacob, *Seek ye me in vain,*
Ifa. 45. 19. Indeed, God is not wanting to his
People in the Ufe of Means : *The Lord is good to*
them that wait for him, to the Soul that feeks him,
Lam. 3. 26. Ordinarily God will not communi-

cate

cate himfelf and his Love any other Way ; and that Soul that negle&ts this, puts himfelf out of the Way of the Manifeftations and Communications of God and his Love: Indeed, God has, as it were, tied himfelf to Souls under a confcienctous Ufe of Means to do them good : *Ask, and you fhall receive, feek, and you fhall find, knock, and it fhall be opened to you : For every one that asketh, receiveth; and every one that feeketh, findeth; and to him that knocketh, it is opened :* As you therefore value Communion with God, and the Manifeftations of his Love, take heed of laying afide the Ufe of Means. —— (Thirdly) Confider, that thefe things we call Means, fuch as Prayer, Hearing, and the like, are Inftances of our Homage, Worfhip, and Obedience, to God , hereby we worfhip God, and give fo far the Glory to him that is due unto his Name , and confequently to caft off thefe, is to caft off the *Worfhip* of God, and to deny we owe Homage to him. Lay all thefe together, and our Propofition is clear, that God's Unchangeablenefs does no way exclude or invalidate the Ufe of Means; and when we ufe Means, 'tis not to change, but fulfil, the Mind of God; 'tis not to alter, but to accomplifh, his Counfels, and bring us into the Fruition of them. Thus by thefe Propofitions I have vindicated the Unchangeablenefs of God from Cavil and Contradi&tion, and it remains a Truth, that the Lord Jehovah is an unchangeable God.

CHAP. VI.

Several Doctrinal Corollaries or Deductions from the Confideration of God's Unchangeablenefs.

HAving thus far afferted, opened, and vindicated, the Unchangeablenefs of God, our next Work shall be to deduce some useful Corollaries or Conclusions thence., and indeed many things of Weight, and very momentous to us, may be drawn from what has been said. As,

1. See here the Glorious Excellency and Perfection of God, and that he is infinitely distinguisht from all the Creatures in Dignity and Glory. God, my Beloved, is every way above, and distinguisht from the Creatures ; He is *the Excellent Glory*, 2 Pet. 1. 17. and there is hardly any thing wherein his Glorious Excellency and Perfection does more brightly, illustriously, and transcendently, appear and shine forth, than in his Unchangeableness. The Creatures are all changeable one way or other, the Heavens and the Earth, with all the Furniture of the one and the other, are changeable ; *they shall perish, yea, all of them shall wax old like a Garment, and be changed as a Vesture*, Psal. 102. 26. The Day is coming wherein *all these shall be dissolved*, 2 Pet. 3. 10, 11. Men also they are changeable, they indeed are Changeableness it self, as it were ; they are changeable in their Nature, and changeable in their Condition ; changeable in their Spirits, and changeable in their Ways ; changeable in their Counsels, and changeable in their Comforts , changeable in all they are , *unstable as Water*, as 'tis said of *Reuben*, Gen. 49. 4. Great Men are changeable, *Psal.* 62. 9. Yea, good Men are changeable, the best Men are changeable, the best Men at their best in this World are changeable , *Verily, every Man at his best Estate is altogether Vanity* , (that is, subject to change) *Ps.* 39. 5. Men are not to Day what they were Yesterday, nor will they be to Morrow what they are to Day, yea, Men are to Day, and to Morrow they are not ; so changeable are they. Yea, the Angels, the Blessed Angels themselves, are changeable ; *God puts no Trust in his Saints, and his Angels he chargeth with*

with *Folly, Job 4, 18* that is, with poſſible, though not actual, Folly; with Change and Folly in their Nature, though not in their Condition: There is, my Beloved, a Peccability in the very Angels, I mean in their Nature. The beſt of Creatures, in themſelves, are ſubject to the worſt of Changes; the Glorious Angels are in their Nature capable of ſinning; indeed, in their Condition they are not, being confirmed in, both all Holineſs and all Happineſs, by the Grace of the Second Covenant, but in their Nature they are: Hence that Saying of one of the School-men, *Whatever Creature there is that is impeccable, and cannot ſin, he has not this from himſelf, or in his Nature, but from the Gift of free Grace.* Thus all the Creatures are changeable, but God is unchangeable, he is for ever the ſame. And O how Glorious does this ſpeak him to be! And how does it diſtinguiſh him from all the Creatures in Perfection and Glory? The Truth is, this is a Glorious Excellency and Perfection in it ſelf, and this puts a Luſtre and Glory upon the Excellencies and Perfections of God; for this (as one ſpeaks) *is an Attribute, which like the Silken String through the Chain of Pearl, runs through all the reſt, and puts a Glory upon all.* God's Holineſs would not be half ſo Glorious, were it not unchangeable Holineſs; his Love would not be half ſo ſweet, were it not unchangeable Love, his Juſtice and Wrath would not be half ſo terrible, were it not unchangeable Juſtice and Wrath: Indeed, what were any of all his Attributes in Compariſon, were they not unchangeable? O! let us learn to ſee and adore God in this Glorious Excellency and Perfection of his.

2. From the Conſideration of God's Unchangeableneſs we conclude the tranſcendent Excellency of Spiritual Things beyond Carnal, Heavenly Things beyond Earthly, and accordingly we

C   ſhould

should prize and pursue the one and the other.
This take for an eternal Rule, That the nearer
things come to God, and the more they resemble
him, and partake of him, the more excellent and
desirable they are. Indeed, as God is the Fountain, so he is the Measure and Standard of all true
Worth and Excellency, and here is nothing that
has any real Worth or Excellency in it, any far-
ther than it resembles him, and partakes of him.
Now what things do most resemble God, and
partake of God? Are they Spiritual or Carnal,
Heavenly or Earthly? Surely Spiritual and Heavenly things, God is unchangeable, and so in their
kind are these · As for Carnal and Earthly things
they are fading and changeable, the best of them
are *Treasures which Moth and Rust doth corrupt, and
which Thieves do break through and steal,* Mat. 6. 19.
They are all fading, dying, transient, things. *The
World passeth away,* (says Saint *John*) 1 *Joh.* 2 17.
that is, fleeting and perishing. 'Tis a good Observation which *Calvin* has upon these· Words,
Because (says he) *in the World there is nothing but
what is fading, and, as it were, but for a Moment,
the Apostle thence concludes, how ill they consult and
provide for themselves, who carve out to themselves
their Happiness here, especially when God calls us to
the Blessed Glory of Eternal Life ; and 'tis as if he
should say, The true Happiness which God offers to his
Children is Eternal, and therefore most unworthy is it
in us to incumber our selves with this World; which,
together with all its good things, will anon vanish
away.* Pray let us lay this Observation to Heart,
The World passeth away; that is, Riches, Honours,
and Pleasures, they all fade and change, are short-
lived: Alas! how soon many times do Riches
change into Poverty, Pleasure into Pain, Honour
into Disgrace and Contempt, Friends into Enemies, Fulness into Want? There is no Stability

in any of these things, they are subject to change every Moment: But now Spiritual and Heavenly things they are lasting and durable, they are *Treasures which neither Moth nor Rust doth corrupt, nor can Thieves break through and steal them,* Mat. 6. 20. The Riches of this World are *uncertain Riches,* vanishing, disappearing, Riches, 1 *Tim.* 6. 17. But the Riches of Heaven, and the Covenant of God's Love, are certain, durable, and abiding, Riches. Grace is a durable thing, the Righteousness of Christ is a durable, unchangeable, Thing; Pardon, Justification, Acceptation with God through that Righteousness, are durable things; Union and Communion with God through Christ, these are unchangeable, these live and last for ever, where attained, and being so, they do come nearer God, they more resemble him, and partake more of him, than Carnal and Earthly things do, and so are more excellent than they, and should be accordingly prized by us. O, my Beloved, there is more true Worth and Excellency in one Dram of Grace, one Beam of Holiness, one Hint of the Pardon of Sin, one Sight of God's reconciled Face, one Imbrace in the Bosom of his Love, than there is in a World of Carnal Comforts and Contentments, and accordingly we should prize and affect them, our Eye and Heart should be taken off from the one, and fixt upon the other. But alas! alas! we are apt to doat upon these changeable things here below · O how fond are we of, and how passionately for the most part are we carried out after, Carnal, Earthly, Sensible, things? But how cold are we in our Love to, and Pursuits after, things Spiritual and Heavenly? As if indeed Earthly, and not Heavenly, things were the only things of Weight and Moment, whereas indeed the one hath no Worth, no Glory, in them, in Comparison of the Glory which excelleth: Let us there-

fore

fore with the Holy Apoftle *not look at the things which are feen, but at the things which are not feen; for the things which are feen are temporal, but the things which are not feen are eternal,* 2 Cor. 4. 18. Mark, the *Apoftle* did not think Carnal and Earthly things worth a Caft of his Eye, becaufe they are temporal, changeable; but Spiritual things, which are durable and eternal, thefe he counted worthy of his Eye, his Heart, and all. O, let us meafure the Worth of things by their Refemblance to God, and what they do partake of him.

3. Behold here, as in a Glafs, the notorious Folly and Madnefs of fuch as prefer the Creature before God, in their Choice and Affections, placing their Happinefs in it, and not in him. *Many* (not one, or two, or a few, but *many*) *fay, Who will fhew us any Good?* And what Good is it they would have fhewn them? *Corn, Wine, Oyl,* Pfal. 4. 6. Creature-good, Senfible-good, Good to feed and fill a fenfual Appetite; and indeed this is the Good which the moft of Men prefer in their Choice and Affections before God, placing the Reft and Happinefs of their Souls therein. The Generality of Men have high Thoughts of the Creature, and low Thoughts of God, great Affections for the Creature, and fmall Affections for God. 'Tis but here and there one that does truly and indeed carry his Happinefs above the Road of Creatures, and place it in God. Take the moft of Men, and 'tis the Creature they Love, 'tis the Creature they prize, 'tis the Creature they chufe, and 'tis the Creature they take up their Reft and Happinefs in; as for God they will have none of him; as God complained of them of old, *Ifrael would none of me,* Pfal. 81. 11. In a Word, God and the Creatures fhare the Hearts and Affections of the whole World between them; God tenders himfelf to Men as the Reft and Happinefs of their

Souls,

Souls, and accordingly to be loved, to be prized, to be chosen, to be delighted in by them, on the other Hand, the Creatures they tender themselves to Men in like manner, and both plead for Acceptation, and which, I pray, carries it, God or the Creature? Truly the Creature with the most: Alas! we are carnal, and senfual, and do naturally incline to carnal and senfual things, embracing them to the Neglect of God, and so the Creature is preferred before God: Oh what Folly and Madness is this! To prefer the Creature before God in our Choice and Affections, is not only to prefer Emptiness before Fulness, Nothingness before Sufficiency, but 'tis also to prefer Vanity before Immutability, and Variableness before Unchangeableness, and Oh, what Folly, what Madness, is this! To prefer the Creature before God in our Choice and Affections, is to prefer a broken Cistern, that can hold no Water, before a Fountain of Living Water. So God himself speaks of it, and withal brands it for a black and horrid Evil, *Jer.* 2. 12, 13. an Evil which he calls upon the Heavens to be astonisht at, and the Earth to be horribly afraid because of. O, my Beloved, to prefer a Cistern before a Fountain; a poor, narrow, scanty, borrowed, Good, before a full, ample, original, all-sufficient, Good, a Drop before an Ocean of Goodness and Sweetness, this is great Folly; but to prefer a broken Cistern, and a broken Cistern that can hold no Water, before a Fountain of Living Waters, fleeting Nothingness before unchangeable Fulness, this is greater Folly, Folly even to Madness, and yet this is the Folly of the most of Men. Carnal Men are often in *Scripture* called Fools, and their Folly appears in nothing more than this, namely, their preferring changeable Creatures before an unchangeable God, and indeed, than this what greater Folly can there be? In

Luke

Luke 12. 19. we read of one that talked to his Soul, faying, *Soul, eat, drink, and be merry, for thou haft much Goods laid up for thee for many Years, take thine Eafe :* Pray mark, he had never a Word of God in his Mouth, and (as we may fafely conclude) never a Thought of God in his Heart, but he was wholly taken up with his Barns, and Goods, and Treafures; and yet he bids his Soul to take its Eafe, to fit down at Reft, God was as nothing with him, and the Creature was all: Well, what Title does Chrift give him? Does he give him the Title of a wife Man? No, *Thou Fool*, (fays he.) Chrift cals him *Fool*, as well he might, for what greater Folly than this, to be wholly taken up with perifhing Creatures, and negleﬅ and forget an unchangeable God? Yea, and to bid his Soul take its Eafe too, becaufe he abounded with Creature enjoyments Indeed, had he faid, Soul, take thine Eafe, be Merry, thou haft Heavenly Treafures laid up in Abundance for thee, God is thine, Chrift is thine, the Bleffed Spirit the Comforter is thine, Heaven and Eternal Life is thine, this had been fomething like, but to have his Heart taken up with carnal things altogether, preferring them before God, and to bid his Soul to reft and be merry upon the Account of thefe, this is Folly with a Witnefs, and who deferves the Name of a Fool, if he did not? What fha'l I fay? This, namely, to prefer the Creature before God, is fuch Folly as will at laft expofe to Shame and Contempt for ever all that are guilty of it, and fuch as are even hung up in Chains for the higheft Inftances of Folly and Madnefs. *Lo,* (fays the *Pfalmift*) *this is the Man that made not God his Strength, but trufted in the Abundance of his Riches*, &c. *Pfal.* 52. 7. Lo, this is the Man that preferred the Creature before God, that made Riches, not God, his Portion; this is that Fool, that very

Fool,

Fool, that mad Man, yea, and whoever they are that do this, they will at laſt (though perhaps too late) ſee and find themſelves to be Fools :- *At his end* (ſays the Prophet concerning ſuch an one) *he ſhall be a Fool*, Jer 17. 11. *at his end he ſhall be a Fool* What, was he a wiſe Man in his Beginning and Progreſs? No, he was a Fool all along, yet though he was a Fool, he thought himſelf wiſe. But at laſt he ſhall ſee his Folly, he ſhall find that he was a very Fool indeed, and O how will the Sight of ſuch Folly then vex and torment him? O, Sirs, when you ſhall ſee your ſelves lanching forth into an unchangeable State, as ſhortly you will, how will you then condemn your ſelves of Folly, for preferring changeable Creatures before an unchangeable God? Let me therefore ſpeak to each of you, as in *Prov.* 23. 5. *Wilt thou ſet thine Eyes upon that which is not? Riches make to themſelves Wings, &c. Ceaſe from thine own Wiſdom, labour not to be Rich* · Men think it to be their higheſt Wiſdom to get· Riches ; but, Sirs, know aſſuredly, this is Folly, the only Wiſdom is to make ſure of God, and get an Intereſt in God, Riches are not, but God always is, and he is the ſame for ever.

4. From God's Unchangeableneſs we infer the abſolute Neceſſity of a Change in Sinners, if ever they be happy, if ever they be ſaved. My Beloved, if ever Sinners be ſaved, and made eternally happy, there muſt be a Change either in God or them; now in God there can be no Change, the Change therefore muſt be in them: 'Tis a rational and undeniable Way of arguing, for a Sinner to argue and ſay, God is unchangeable, and becauſe God is unchangeable, I muſt change or. periſh, change or die, change or be miſerable for ever For pray mark, God never did, and he never will, ſave any Man in his Sins, he is in Chriſt infinitely willing, ready, and able, to ſave Men

C 4 from

from their Sins, he fent and feal'd his Son on
purpofe to fave Men from their Sins, and accord
ingly gave him a Name fuitable hereunto, even
Jefus, which fignifies a Saviour, *Thou fhalt call his*
Name Jefus, for he fhall fave his People from their
Sins, Mat. 1. 21. But he never did, and unlefs he
fhould change, he never will, fave any in their
Sins, without a Change therefore in us and upon
us we are undone for ever. But a little further,
yet to let you fee the Force of this Inference, and
the Rationality of fuch an arguing, that fo it may
fall with the greater Weight and Conviction upon
all our Sou's, be pleafed to confider that 'tis utterly repugnant to, and inconfiftent with, the
Word, Nature, Counfel, and Oath, of God, to
fave Sinners without a Change, for all thefe are
abfolutely and exprefly againft the Happinefs and
Salvation of unchanged Souls, Souls remaining ftill
in their Sins, ftill in their natural State.

1 The Word of God is againft the Happinefs
and Salvation of unchanged Souls; the Word of
God fays exprefly, that without a Change Men
may not, fhall not, cannot, be faved; the Word
of God fays, *The Wicked fhall be turned into Hell,*
and all that forget God, Pfal. 9. 17. The Word
of God fays, *that into the Holy City there fhall in no*
wife enter any thing that defileth or worketh Abomina-
tion, Rev. 21. 27. The Word of God fays, *That*
the Unrighteous fhall not inherit the Kingdom of God,
1 *Cor.* 6. 9. The Word of God fays, *That with-*
out Holinefs no Man fhall fee God, Heb. 12. 14. And
left all this fhould be thought to concern only
profane and licentious ones, let me add, the
Word of God fays, that *Flefh and Blood, that is,*
Men in their natural Eftate, *cannot enter into the*
Kingdom of God, 1 *Cor.* 15. 50. Yea, the Word
of God fays, and that with an Emphafis, that *ex-*
cept a Man be born again, unlefs he be regenerated

by

by the Spirit, *he cannot enter into the Kingdom of Heaven,* Joh. 3. 3, 5. *Verily, verily,* (says Chriſt) *except a Man be born again,* &c. and again, *Verily, verily,* he aſſerts it over and over, which notes, among other things, as the Weight of the Truth aſſerted, ſo our Difficulty and Averſeneſs to believe it, and bow to it. Thus the Word of God is againſt this thing.

2. The Nature of God is againſt the Happineſs and Salvation of unchanged Souls; the Nature of God is infinitely Pure and Holy, and will not admit of Sinners to dwell with him: *Thou art not a God that hath Pleaſure in Wickedneſs,* (ſays the Pſalmiſt) *neither ſhall Evil dwell with thee,* Pſal. 5. 4. *The Fooliſh* (and ſuch are all Men by Nature) *ſhall not ſtand in thy Sight, thou hateſt all the Workers of Iniquity, v.* 5. So *Heb.* 1. 13. *Thou art of purer Eyes than to behold Evil, and canſt not look on Iniquity;* that is, without Loathing and Deteſtation: God's Nature is Holy, yea, 'tis Holineſs it ſelf, and he can as ſoon ceaſe to be God, as ceaſe to be Holy; his Nature is infinitely contrary to all Sin, and he infinitely, neceſſarily, and eternally, hates all Sin, Sin indeed is ſtrictly and properly the only Object of God's Hatred: His Love is let out upon many Objects, but Sin is the only Object of his Hatred; and is not the Nature of this God againſt the Salvation of unchanged Sinners? God muſt firſt ceaſe to be infinitely Holy, and ſo to be God, e'er Sinners remaining in their unchanged State can be ſaved.

3. The Counſel of God is againſt the Salvation of unchanged Souls, the Law of the Counſel of God is, That we muſt be holy if ever we will be happy, that we muſt be called, juſtified, and ſanctified, if ever we be glorified; ſo you find in that Golden Chain, (as 'tis called) *Rom.* 8. 29, 30. *Whom he did foreknow, he alſo did preſeſtinate to be*

C 5 *conformed t*

conformed unto the Image of his Son. Moreover, *whom he did predestinate, them he also called, and whom he called, them he also justified, and whom he justified, them he also glorified* Mark, the Counsel, or as 'tis here called, the Fore-knowledge, of God, tells us, we must be changed, called, and justified, if ever we be glorified. So expresly, 2 *Thes.* 2. 13. *God hath chosen us to Salvation :* But how? Is there no need of a Change? Yes, he hath so chosen us, as calls for a Change ; *He hath chosen us to Salvation, through the Sanctification of the Spirit, and Belief of the Truth :* Yea, the Counsel of God aims at Holiness, and designs us primarily unto Holiness; *He hath chosen us that we should be holy,* *Eph* 1. 4, 5. God must change all his Counsels which have been of old, or Sinners must be changed, if ever they be saved.

4 The Oath of God is against the Salvation of unchanged Sinners: God's Oath is gone out of his Mouth, that no unbelieving, unchanged, ones, shall ever enter into his Rest *So I sware in my Wrath they shall not enter into my Rest,* Heb. 3. 11. Thus God's Word, his Nature, his Counsel, his Oath, are all against the Happiness and Salvation of unchanged Sinners, and God must change in all, if ever they be saved without a Change. But God can change in neither ; the Change must be in them; God being unchangeable, they must change or die, change or perish, and there must be a double Change pass upon them, or they cannot be saved, a Change of their Estate, and a Change of their Image, a Change of their State in Justification by the Blood of Christ, and a Change of their Image in Regeneration and Sanctification by the Spirit of Christ, and without both these they are undone for ever.

1. There must be a Change of their State in Justification through Christ's Blood, if ever they be saved. When a poor Soul is justified freely by Grace,
through.

through the Redemption that is in Jeſus, as the Apoſtle expreſſes it, *Rom.* 3. 24. when his Sins are once pardoned, and his Perſon accepted with God by the Imputation of Chriſt's perfect Righteouſneſs to him, through believing, then is his State changed, and this Change of State Sinners muſt paſs under, or God being unchangeable, they cannot be ſaved, they muſt, through the Blood and Righteouſneſs of Chriſt applied and appropriated in a way of believing, get their Sins pardoned, and their Perſons accepted, they muſt get all Guilt removed, and all Debts paid, or they cannot poſſibly be ſaved ; this is frequently mentioned in Scripture, *Rom.* 5. 1. *Being juſtified by Faith, we have Peace with God through our Lord Jeſus Chriſt.* Again, *v.* 9. *Being juſtified through his Blood, we ſhall be ſaved from Wrath by him ;* Again, *v.* 17, 18, 19. *If by one Man's Offence Death reigned by one, much more they which receive abundance of Grace, and of the Gift of Righteouſneſs, ſhall reign in Life by one, Jeſus Chriſt · Therefore, as by the Offence of one Judgment came upon all Men to Condemnation, ſo by the Obedience of one ſhall many be made Righteous.* Still you ſee Juſtification through the Blood and Righteouſneſs of Chriſt is neceſſary unto Life and Salvation. So *Eph.* 1. 6, 7. *God hath made us accepted in the Beloved, in whom we have Redemption through his Blood, even the Forgiveneſs of Sins :* The like is held forth, 1 *Cor.* & 10. *&c.* 8. 30. Oh, without Pardon and Juſtification through the Blood of Chriſt, there is no Life, no Salvation, to be expected for Sinners : Unpardoned Sin will ſurely damn, and no Pardon is to be had for Sinners but in and by Chriſt, and Union with Chriſt, through believing. When once a Soul is pardoned and juſtified by Chriſt through believing, then he is *paſſed from Death to Life,* as you have it, *Joh* 5. 24. but till then he remains in Death, and under Death and Condemnation. 2. Theſſa.

2. There muſt be a Change of their Image in Regeneration and Sanctification by the Spirit of Chriſt. When a Sinner is new born, *born of Water and of the Spirit*, as Chriſt's Expreſſion is, when he is made *a new Creature, old things being paſt away with him, and all things being become new,* as the Apoſtle phraſes it, 2 *Cor.* 5. 17. when he is *created in Chriſt Jeſus,* and has a ſound Work of Grace wrought and carried on in him by the Spirit of Chriſt, then is his Image changed, and ſuch a Change of Image muſt Sinners paſs under; or they cannot be ſaved God never did, and never will, ſave an unrenewed Soul, his Unchangeableneſs will not admit of the Salvation of ſuch an one ; and indeed the Scripture is full in it, *Joh.* 3. 3, 5. *Verily, verily,* (ſays Chriſt to *Nicodemus)* ex- *cept a Man be born again, he cannot ſee the Kingdom of God :* And again, *verſ.* 5. *Verily, verily,* (ſays he) *except a Man be born of Water, and of the Spirit, he cannot enter into the Kingdom of God.* You ſee this is what Chriſt aſſerts, and that over and over, and with the higheſt Aſſeverations imagina ble : Hence alſo Heaven is ſaid to be *the Inheritance of Saints, Col.* 1. 12. and of *ſanctified Ones, Acts* 26. 18. Hence the *Corinthians* are ſaid to be *ſanctified* as well as *juſtified,* and ſo made capable of inheriting the Kingdom of God, 1 *Cor.* 6. 10, 11. and *Tit.* 3. 5. God is ſaid, *according to his Mercy to ſave us, by the waſhing of Regeneration, and the renewing of the Holy Ghoſt.* Thus there muſt a Change of Image as well as State paſs upon us, or we cannot be ſaved; and that becauſe God is un changeable Oh, how ſhould we all therefore look after this Change ? Soul, aſſure thy ſelf, 'tis not thy Civility and Morality, how much ſoever raiſed and refined, 'tis not thy external Reforma tions, 'tis not thy conforming thy ſelf to the out ward Rules and Laws of Duty, and the like, that will

4

will fave thee, or avail thee any thing as to eternal Life, unlefs thou comeft under this double Change, of which thou haft heard. *Paul*, I am confident, could compare with thee for Morality and external Conformity to the Law, when yet he was in a loft Eftate ; and afterwards coming to Faith in Chrift, he fees Caufe *to account all but as Lofs and Dung*, Phil. 3. *begin.* And he that came to Chrift, (of whom we read in *Mat.* 19. 16, 17, 18, 19, 20, 21, 22.) had certainly attained to a great Degree of Morality, and external Conformity to the Law, who yet was lacking, and fo far lacking, as that, for any thing we find, he fell eternally fhort of Heaven and Salvation. Oh, there muft a Change, a Change of State, and a Change of Image, pafs upon us, or our Morality will leave us at laft to perifh : Let us therefore mind this Change : Am I changed or no? Changed I muft be, and that with a great Change, with a Change of State, and a Change of Perfon, or I cannot be faved , have I therefore any Acquaintance with fuch a Change? O, my Beloved, let Unchangeablenefs in God ingage us all to look out after a Change in us, God will not change to fave any of us all, he is willing to change us that we may be faved, but he himfelf will not change to fave any of us.

5. Again, from what has been declared touching God's Unchangeablenefs, we conclude and infer the infinite Sweetnefs of his Love, and the infinite Bitternefs of his Wrath, and fo the exceeding Happinefs of fuch as are interefted in the one, and the extream Mifery of fuch as fall under the other. Sinners flight God's Love, preferring Creature love before it, and they difregard his Wrath, wilfully provoking it againft themfelves , but if they will view the one and the other, in the Glafs of his Unchangeablenefs, they will find that there

is more Sweetnefs in the one than that it fhould
be flighted; and more Terriblenefs in the other,
than that it fhould be difregarded.

1. From God's Unchangeablenefs we conclude
and infer the Infinite Sweetnefs of his Love, and
fo the Happinefs of them that are interefted in it.
God has a People whom he loves, and his Love to
them is a free Love, a rich Love, a peculiar Love,
a Love of fingular Eminency and Perfection in all
Refpects: But that which indeed crowns all, and
puts an infinite Sweetnefs into it, is this, that tis
an unchangeable Love, a Love that never fades,
never varies: True, his Love may be, and fometimes is, vailed and clouded, but tho' it be vailed,
yet 'tis not varied, though it be fometimes clouded, yet 'tis never changed. Love, under a Vail or
Cloud, is Love. The Sun may be under a Cloud,
yea, there may be an Eclipfe upon it for a time,
which may keep it out of our View, and deprive
us of the comfortable Influences and Shinings of
it for a Seafon; but yet even then the Sun is in
Being, and after a while in will fhine again, and
that as fweetly, brightly, and comfortably, as
ever. So there may be a Vail, a Cloud, an E-
clipfe, as it were, upon God's Love, fuch as may
deprive us for a time of the comfortable Views,
Shinings, and Influences, of it. But yet even
then 'tis Love, and fweet Love too, and after a
while it will fhine and fhew it felf again. 'Tis a
fweet Word which you have. *Pfal.* 30. 5. *His An-*
ger endureth but a Moment, in his Favour is Life:
Weeping may endure for a Night, but Joy comes in the
Morning · In his Favour is Life. Life here (as a Judicious Interpreter obferves) is oppofed to a Moment, mentioned in the Beginning of the Verfe,
and fo the Senfe is, that that Love, wherewith
G d loves his People, lafts throughout all Life, it
lives and lafts for ever, 'tis a durable, abiding, Love:
So

So *Ifa.* 54. 8. *In a little Wrath I hid my Face from thee for a Moment*, (fays God to his Church) *but with everlafting Kindnefs will I have Mercy on thee.* Thus I fay, though God's Love to his People may be vailed, yet 'tis never varied, 'tis a conftant Love, and Oh how fweet does this fpeak his Love to be, and how happy are they that are interefted in it? Oh, to be beloved by an unchangeable God, with an unchangeable Love, this is fweet indeed! The Creature's Love has little Worth or Sweetnefs in it, and that not only becaufe of its Weaknefs and Emptinefs, but alfo becaufe of its Changeablenefs: Alas! The Creature loves to Day, and hates to Morrow, Oh, but now God's Love is another manner of Love, a Love that has Fulnefs and Firmnefs, Sufficiency and Immutability, both in it; and accordingly muft needs be infinitely fweet and defirable. Well therefore might *David* admiringly cry out as he did, *Pfal.* 36. 7. *How excellent or how precious is thy Loving kindnefs, O Lord?* And as in Pfal. 63. 3. *Thy Loving-kindnefs is better than Life:* 'Tis before all Lives, one Dram of it is to be preferred before many Worlds of Creature injoyments. God's Love, it is all Good, all Comfort, ad Happinefs, in its Fountain-fulnefs and Purity; it is an eternal, never failing, Spring of Sweetnefs, an unvariable Fountain of Delight; in it there is Grace, all Grace, Peace, all Peace, Joy, all Joy; Satisfaction, all Satisfaction; Reft and Solace, all Reft and Solace: O, Soul, look upon the Love of thy God to thee, look upon it, and in it thou wilt fee unfearchable Riches, unmeafurable Fulnefs, unfathomable Depths, and (which crowns all) eternal Unchangeablenefs, and Oh how happy wilt thou therein fee thy felf! With what full Confolation of Spirit mayeft thou fit down and fay, God loves me, and he loves me unchangeably. Friends change, outward Comforts change,

I.

I my felf change , but God's Love to me changes
not; I am for ever upon his Heart, nor can either
Men or Devils, Sins or Sorrows, caſt me out of it.
True, he ſometimes afflicts me, but yet he loves
me ; he ſometimes frowns upon me, but yet he
loves me ; he ſometimes ſeems to ſlay me, he
breaks me with Breach upon Breach, but yet he
loves me , he confines me to a Sick chamber, he lays
me upon a Sick bed, he ſeems to reſolve to lay
me in the Duſt, but yet he loves me ; yea, all
this is in Love . I break with him, and depart
from him, I am ſinning againſt him every Day and
Hour, but yet he loves me, he loves me notwith-
ſtanding all, his Love cannot be broken off from
me, and after a while I ſhall bathe in the Fountain
thereof for ever. Oh ſweet! Who would not long
for this Love ? He loves me unchangeably, and he
will therefore cleanſe me, purifie me, pardon me,
make me perfectly Holy He loves me, and he will
love me, till he has lodged me in his own *Preſence*
and *Boſom* above, and there he will love me for
ever.

2. From God's Unchangeableneſs, we conclude
and infer the Infinite Bitterneſs of his Wrath, and
the extream Miſery of all ſuch as fall under the
Weight thereof. God's Love is not more ſweet
than his Wrath is bitter, his Love is not more deſirable than his Wrath is formidable, and that becauſe he is an unchangeable God ; and Oh how
miſerab'e muſt they be that do fall under this
Wrath. In *Iſa.* 10 6. we read of *the People of
God's Wrath:* There are ſome then that are properly *the People of God's Wrath*, they are *Children
of Wrath, Heirs of Wrath;* and Wrath, yea, God's
Wrat! , will be their Portion for ever ; ſuch are
all finally impenitent and unbelieving Ones, all
who live and die in their Impenitency and Unbelief, and Oh how extreamly miſerable muſt they
be !

be! God's Wrath is a *Great Wrath, a Fierce Wrath, a Sore Wrath, a Powerful Wrath,* an *Irrefiftable Wrath, a Burning, Confuming, and Devouring, Wrath*; fo the Scripture fpeaks of it. All which fpeaks the exceeding Bitternefs and Terriblenefs of it, and the extream Mifery of fuch as fall under it, but that which adds even infinitely to all this, that 'tis eternal and unchangeable Wrath, Wrath that abides for ever. Hence 'tis fet forth in Scripture by *unquenchable Fire, Mat.* 3. 12. God's Wrath is called *Fire,* becaufe of its exceeding Heat and Fiercenefs, being of a confuming and devouring Nature, and 'tis called *unquenchable Fire,* becaufe 'tis durable and unchangeable, it being what admits of no more Change or Period than his Love does, and to fall under this unquenchable Fire, under the Revelation of this eternal, unchangeable, Wrath, - Oh how fad, how miferable, muft this be? *Solomon* tells us, that *the Wrath of a King is as the Rowing of a Lion, Prov.* 19. 12. and what then, and how terrible, is the Wrath of God, to whofe Wrath the Wrath of all the Kings on the Earth is as nothing? We are afraid fometimes of Man's Wrath, yea, fo afraid of it, as to fuffer our felves to be driven from our Duty by it. But, my Beloved, what is the Wrath of a Man to the Wrath of God? What is the Wrath of a changeable Man to the Wrath of an unchangeable God? Let me fay to each Soul of you, as God by the Prophet to them, *Ifa.* 51. 12, 13. *Who art thou that thou fhouldeft be afraid of a Man that fhall die,* (a changeable Creature) *and forgetteft the Lord thy Maker?* 'Tis but a little while, and Man and his Wrath both fhall change and die, but God and his Wrath will live for ever: O, learn to fear and tremble at his Wrath, and beware how for a little fading, changeable, Delight in Sin, you throw your felves under unchangeable Wrath and Fury : Poor
Sinner,

Sinner, thou makeſt light of God's Wrath, as if
it were an inconſiderable toing, witneſs thy wil-
ful and daily Provoking of it againſt thee by Sin,
witneſs thy Inſenſibleneſs of and under the Tokens
and Revelations of it, witneſs thy Neglect of
Chriſt, and of making thy Peace with God by him,
and the like · But, Soul, view it in the Glaſs of
his infinite Unchangeableneſs, and then ſee whether it be a thing to be made light of or no; the
Saints they tremble but in the Apprehenſion of it,
Who knows the Power of thine Anger? ſays *Moſes*,
Pſal. 90 11. They ſigh, they bleed, they groan,
yea, they die, and are even diſtracted under a little temporal Sprinklings and Droppings of it, *Pſal.*
88. 15, 16. yea, they dread and tremble many
times at but the Revelation of it againſt others, *I
was afraid* (ſays *Moſes) of the Anger and hot Diſ-
pleaſure wherewith the Lord was wrath againſt you,
to deſtroy you, Deut.* 9. 19. *Moſes* cou'd contemn
the Wrath of Man, yea, of Man whoſe Wrath of all
Men is moſt terrible, the Wrath of a King, *Heb.*
11. 27. but yet he trembles at the Wrath of God,
when 'twas provoked againſt others, thus the
Saints tremble at God's Wrath: Yea, more, the
Devils themſelves do dread and tremble at Gods
Wrath, *The Devils believe and tremble,* Jam. 2 19.
they believe there is a God, and they tremble at
the Apprehenſion of the Wrath of that God. And,
Sinner, whoever thou art, how light ſoever thou
mayeſt now make of God's Wrath, yet know that
there is a time coming when thou and the ſtouteſt
Sinners in the World muſt and will tremble at it.
See that one Text, *Iſa* 33. 14 *The Sinners in Sion
are afraid, Fearfulneſs hath ſurprized the Hypocrite:*
Why, what is the matter? Verily nothing but the
Sight and Apprehenſion of God's Wrath and Vengeance coming upon them, ſo much the follow
ing Words ſhew, *Who among us ſhall dwell with de-*
vouring

vouring Fire? Who amongst us shall dwell with everlasting Burnings? They saw God's Wrath to be as
a devouring Fire, they saw the Terror of it in the
Glass of God's Unchangeableness, and therefore
call it *everlasting Burnings*, and this filled them
with Dread and Trembling. Take one Place more,
Rev 6. 15, 16, 17. in *verf.* 16, 17. we find some
*crying out to the Mountains and Rocks to fall on them,
and hide them from the Face of him that sitteth upon
the Throne, and from the Wrath of the Lamb, for
(*say they*) the great Day of his Wrath is come, and
who shall be able to stand?* Well, but who are they
that thus cry out? Surely they are only a Compa-
ny of low spirited Creatures, thinkest thou, they
are only some Women and Children, or some base
cowardly Ones, that never had the Spirit and Courage of Men. No, Soul, they are no such Persons, they are *the Kings of the Earth, and the great
Men, and the rich Men, and the chief Captains, and
the mighty Men, and every Bond-man, and every Free-
man*, all Sorts of Men, Men of the highest Place,
the highest Estates, the highest Courage and Va-
lour, as well as others, these all are said *to hide
themselves in the Dens and in the Rocks of the Mountains, and call unto the Mountains and Rocks, saying,
Fall on us.* Oh, but we shall fall heavy, no matter, fall on us, but to what Purpose? Why, *to
hide us from the Wrath of God*, why, what is the
Matter? Are you afraid of the Wrath of God?
Time was you slighted and disregarded it as an in-
confiderable thing, and do you so dread it now,
and tremble at it now, that you cry to us Rocks
and Mountains to fall on you, to hide you from
it? Oh yes, good Rocks, good Mountains, fall on
us, you will lye light and easie upon us in
Comparison of what the Wrath of God will do.
How? Why should you think so? You had other
Thoughts of God's Wrath a while ago, why do
you

you fo dread it and tremble at it now? O, becaufe *the great Day of his Wrath is come, and none
can ftand before it,* fay they   We lookt on this
Wrath a while ago at a Diftance, and then it
feemed a light thing, but now *the Day,* yea, *the
great Day, of his Wrath is come,* and there is no
ftanding for us   While we lookt at it at a Diftance,
we could ftand before it, and make light of it;
yea, in fome leffer Days of Wrath we have born
up well enough, but now his Wrath is come near
us, yea, and the Fulnefs and Fiercenefs of it is
breaking forth againft us, now we fee this Wrath
to be more dreadful and formidable, and that we
can never ftand up either under it or againft it:
Say ye fo, reply the Rocks and Mountains, then
no wonder you cry to us to hide you from it, but
truly 'tis more than we can do for you, you muft
now bear and grapple with that Wrath for ever,
as to any Relief we can afford you in the Cafe.   O
Sinner! when the great Day of God's Wrath fhall
come. then, if not before, thou alfo wilt tremble
at his Wrath   Indeed now wouldeft thou fee it,
and tremb'e at it, thou mighteft cry to a Rock
that could and would hide thee from it, provided
thou gettreft into it, I mean *Chrift, that Rock of Ages,*
he being embraced by Faith, and thy Soul having
Union with him, would hide and fecure thee
againft the Wrath of God for ever, but if thou
wilt go on to make light of this Wrath, and to
provoke it daily againft thee by Sin, thou wilt at
laft fink under the Weight and Burthen thereof
for ever.

6. In the Glafs of God's Unchangeablenefs we
fee the true Reafon why the beft of us all are not
confumed, and accordingly let us give the Glory
of it where 'tis due. Beloved, why are you, and
I, and others, not confumed? True, we meet
with fome Afflictions, and are exercifed with fome
Difficulties

Difficulties now and then, but why are we not utterly conſumed and deſtroyed? Verily, 'tis not becauſe we are able to ſave our ſelves, nor is it becauſe we deſerve that God ſhould ſave us, but 'tis purely and ſolely becauſe our God is unchangeable. This Account the Text it ſelf gives of it; *I am the Lord, I change not; therefore ye Sons of Jacob are not conſumed:* All our Security lyes in God's Immutability, we periſh not, becauſe he changes not: Pray give me leave a little to be free with you and my ſelf, why are we not conſumed with an external Conſumption? We are ſorely broken many of us, 'tis true, we are broken in our Eſtates, in our Healths, in our Comforts, in our Relations, but why are we not utterly deſtroyed? Why are we alive? Why have we any one Comfort about us? Yea more, why are we not conſumed with an eternal Conſumption? Why are the beſt of us all not in Hell? Why are we not ſtated in an Eternity of Woe and Miſery? Why are we not now roaring and ſweltering under the Wrath of God? Why are we not Companions with Devils and damned Spirits in everlaſting Burnings? Is it becauſe our Sins are few and ſmall, and have not deſerved it? No ſurely; why then is it? Becauſe our God is unchangeable, unchangeable in Being, Counſel, Covenant, and Love. Oh! my Beloved, if we ſeriouſly conſider what we are, and how we have carried it, what our Sins and Provocations have been, and how high they riſe againſt the Bleſſed God, and the like, we may well wonder we are out of Hell, that we have a Being any where on this ſide the Pit of Perdition, nor can we reſolve it into any other Cauſe but God's Unchangeableneſs. Let me therefore entreat you to conſider things a little, that you may give Glory where 'tis due.

1. Conſider

1. Confider what you are, I mean as to your Nature and the Depravednefs of it: You are a meer Lump and Mafs of Sin, *Enemies*, yea, *Enmi ty it felt againft God* and Chrift, *Rom.* 8. 7 your Heart is a meer Sink, a Fountain, an Abyfs, of Sin and Wickednefs againft God: *The Heart is de- ceitful above all things, and defperately wicked, who can know it?* None but God can look to the Bottom of that Sin, Wickednefs, and Deceit, that is in your Heart, *Jer.* 17. 9. O the Aboundings of Sin that are found in the beft of us! Oh, the Pride, the Paffion, the Earthlinefs, the Senfua lity, the Uncleannefs, the Unbelief, the Hypocri- fie, the Atheifm, the Difregard of God, the A verfion from all Good, that dwells, works, wars, and oftentimes prevails and predominates, in the Hearts of the beft Saints, while here! O the Ri fings of Sin, and Oh the Aboundings of Iniquity, that are found among us!

2. Confider what you have done, and how you have carried it God-ward: If you ferioufly con- fider things, you will find, I fear, that you have done, and to this Day do, little elfe but fin againft the Lord: You have defpifed his Goodnefs, abu fed his Love, violated his Laws, trampled upon his Authority, grieved his Spirit, wounded his Son, darkned his Glory, and oftentimes ftruck even at his very Crown and Being, yea, and *this hath been your manner from your Youth*, (as God charged them of old, *Jer.* 22. 21.) there is not that Day, nor fcarcely that Hour, wherein you have not, and do not, fin againft God: Often *have you made him ferve with your Sins, and wearied him with your Iniquities*, as thofe, *Ifa.* 43. 24. Your Lives have been Lives of Sin for the moft part againft God.

3. Confider what black and horrid Aggravations your Sins are cloathed with, are not your Sins, my Beloved, of a Scarlet Dye, and Crimfon Tin-

cture

fure? Are they not heightened with many black and crying Aggravations? Have they not, at leaft many of them, been committed againft much Love, much Light, much Mercy, many Motions of the Spirit, many Checks of Confcience, many Bonds and Obligations to Duty, many fignal and eminent Appearances, of God to you, and for you, many Taftes, many Sealings, of his Love, and the like? What fhall I fay? Such every way are our Sins, yea, the Sins of the beft of us all, that we cannot poffibly look to the further end of them. *Who can underftand his Errors?* (fays Holy *David,* Pfal. 19. 12.) *David* was an Holy Man, *a Man after God's own Heart,* and yet he cries out, *Who can underftand his Errors?* His Sins were beyond Search or Underftanding; and if his were fo, what are ours? Truly, my Beloved, our Sins in the Number, Nature, and Aggravations, of them, are beyond our Reach, and well may we all with him cry out, *Who can underftand his Errors?*

4. Confider what an infinite Evil and Demerit there is in every Sin, even the leaft Sin? As you are guilty of fo much Sin, and your Sins cloathed many of them with fo many and fuch crying Aggravations, fo you muft know that there is Evil enough in the leaft Sin to damn you eternally, fhould God render the Defert thereof to you: *The Wages of Sin is Death,* (fays the Apoftle) *Rom.* 6. 23. Mark, he fpeaks of *Sin* indefinitely, every *Sin,* the leaft *Sin*; and, fays he, *the Wages,* that which is due to it, *is Death:* Every Sin is an Offence againft God, 'tis infinitely contrary to his Purity and Holinefs, his Will and Glory, his Life and Being; 'tis univerfally contrary to him, and fo muft needs have an inconceivable Evil and Demerit in it: *Every Offence* (fays a Learned Man) *againft the chief Good, deferves the utmoft Punifh-ment, even the eternal Deftruction of the Creature.* O, Sirs,

Sirs, we little think the Evil there is in a vain Thought, an idle Word, an unholy, irregular, Action. We little think the Evil the least Sin carries in it.

5. Consider how much God hates Sin : Sin is even infinitely odious and abominable to him, *God is of purer Eyes than to behold Iniquity,* to wit, without Loathing and Detestation, *Hab.* 1. 13. and he is once and again in Scripture represented as a God hating Sin ; Sin indeed is infinitely odious in his Sight. Now let us weigh these things, and lay them together, and then we shall see that it can be nothing else that keeps us from Destruction but God's Unchangeableness, to which therefore we should give the Glory: 'Tis the Grace and Love of God that first brings us into a Condition of Life and Salvation, and 'tis the Unchangeableness of God that keeps us there. Truly, when some of us reflect a little upon our selves, and consider what we are, and have been, in our Spirits and Carriages God-ward; how much we have provoked him, what frequent Forfeitures we have made, and do make, of our Lives, Souls, and all, we see infinite Cause to wonder that we are alive, that the Flames of Divine Wrath had not long since kindled upon us, and the Revenges of Divine Justice broken out against us, and blessed be God that we are out of Hell. O, that such a proud, such a stubborn, such a stiff-necked, People, as we are, should yet live! That Persons of so many and high Provocations against God, as thou Reader, and I, are guilty of, should yet have a Being out of Hell ! This is solely from the Unchangeableness of God : And, my Beloved, we do not rightly consider the Matter if we do not see and acknowledge it to be so. O blessed be God for his Unchangeableness ! had not God been unchangeable, where had I now been ? I had now been shut up

in the Infernal Pit, I had now been a Companion
with Devils and Damned Spirits, I had now been
feparated from God for ever; and how miferable
then had I been? O, my Soul, adore the Unchangeable One, and blefs him for his Unchangeable
Counfel, his Unchangeable Covenant, his Un
changeable Love.

CHAP. VII.

*Several Grounds of Humbling from the Confideration
of God's Unchangeablenefs, as our Unlikerefs to him
therein, our charging him with Change, our living
fo little upon his Unchangeablenefs.*

AS the Unchangeablenefs of God is very Teaching and Inftructive, fo alfo very Humbling,
if rightly weighed and improved by us: There are
feveral Things which the Confideration thereof do
call aloud upon us to be humbled for, and Oh that
we would lay them to Heart!

1. Is God unchangeable? Then how fhould we
be humbled for our exceeding great Changeablenefs and therein our Unlikenefs to God the Chief
Good? The more changeable we are in what is
good, the more unlike God we are; and the more
unlike God we are, the more Caufe we have of
humbling. Oh, how fhould we loath our felves,
and be abafed at the Foot of God in the Senfe of
our great Ficklenefs and Changeablenefs? Alas!
how changeable are we in all that is good? How
changeable are many of us in our Judgments and
Opinions, being *like Children toffed to and fro, and
had about with every Wind of Doctrine,* as you

D

have

have it, *Eph.* 4 14. being apt *to be soon removed from the Faith of the Gospel,* as the *Galatians* were, at which *Paul marvelled, Gal.* 1. 6. How change-able are we in our Affections to God, and the Things of God? Now the Heart flames with Love to God and Christ, anon 'tis chill and cold. Now we are full of Holy Longings and Desires after God, and Christ, Grace, and Glory, we can say with the Church of old, *The Desire of our Soul is unto thee, O God, and to the Remembrance of thy Name, Isa.* 26. 8. yea, *our Soul thirsteth for God, yea, for the Living God,* yea, *as the Hart panteth after the Water-brooks, so panteth our Soul after God,* as the *Psalmist* speaks. Anon there is not any one Holy Breathing to be found within us: No, we are even made up of worldly, sinful, unclean, De-sires, *we pant after the Dust of the Earth,* as those, *Amos* 2. 7. we are athirst for the Creature, and nothing but that will satisfie us. Now we delight in God and his Ways, *We rejoice in the Lord, and our Soul is joyful in our God,* as 'twas with the Church, *Isa.* 61. 10. and his Ways are sweet and pleasant to us, his Law is our Delight; anon we relish no Sweetness, we take and exercise no Joy, no Delight, either in the one or in the other; but we drive on heavily, every Duty being a Burthen to us, and the very Thoughts of God a Trouble. Now we fear and stand in awe of God, not da-ring to sin against him, we stand in awe of his Pre-sence, we stand in awe of his Holiness, we stand in awe of his Goodness, we stand in awe of his Power, and the like. Anon we are fearless and regardless of him, boldly venturing upon sinning against him Now we dread Sin as Hell it self, yea, and worse too; anon we embrace it, and de-light in it. Again, how changeable are we in our Holy Purposes and Resolutions? We take up this and that Holy Resolution, we purpose to walk so and

and ſo with God, to keep ſuch and ſuch a Watch over our Spirits and Ways; to live more in Communion with God, to drive a greater Trade and Deſign to Heaven, and to haſten more to that better Country, and the like, but alas! how do ſuch Reſolutions fade, and change, and die, within us, not one of many of them ever proves firm and effectual, yea, many times no ſooner are ſuch Reſolutions taken up by us, but preſently we run counter to them, and break with God more than before, the firſt Temptation that comes turns us quite beſide our Purpoſe, and we miſerably miſcarry in the very things we reſolved about: Our Holy Purpoſes are for the moſt part abortive, *We turn aſide like a deceitful Bow*, (as God complains of thoſe, *Pſal.* 78. 57.) 'Tis a ſad Complaint which I have read in one of the Ancients, *Oftentimes* (ſays he) *have I promiſed and reſolved to amend, but I never made it good, but always I returned to Sin, and to my former Wickedneſſes, I added new, and worſe, I never reformed as I ought.* And who of us may not in a great Meaſure make the ſame Complaint? Yet once more, how changeable are we in our Ways and Walkings? How uneven and unconſtant in our Goings? We have *an Heart that loveth to wander,* (as God ſpeaks of them of old, *Jer.* 14. 10.) O the Turnings aſide, and O the Turnings back, that we are guilty of in our walking with God! Oh the Gaps, and Pauſes, and Interruptions, that are in our Obedience! we ſhould go on in one even conſtant Tenure of Holy Obedience, but alas! we are in and out, off and on, often in the Day, yea, in the Hour; yea, many times ſudden and great Changes are found in our Spirits and Carriages God-ward, and that for the worſe. I'll give you one, and but one, Inſtance of this, and that in an eminently Holy Man, an Inſtance that may well make all of us tremble, and

D 2

that

that is of *Jeremiah*, Jer. 20. 13, 14, 15. *Sing un-*
to the Lord, praise ye the Lord ; for he hath delivered
the Soul of the Poor from the Hand of Evil-doers.
Cursed be the Day wherein I was born , let not the
Day wherein my Mother bare me be blessed. Cursed
be the Man that brought Tidings to my Father, saying,
A Man-child is born unto thee, making him very glad.
Pray mark, what a great Change there was wrought
in this Good Man's Spirit, and that all of a sudden;
in *Verf.* 13. he looks like one dropt out of Heaven,
praising God for his Goodness and Salvation, and
calling upon others so to do , but in *Verf.* 14, 15,
he looks rather like one broken loose out of Hell
curfing himself, and almost every one about him.
In the one he looks more like an Angel than an
imperfect Saint , in the other he looks more like
a Devil than a Man , so great was the Change in
his Spirit, and this suddenly made. When he had
in *Verf.* 13. been praising God, and was, as it
were, taken up to Heaven, the very next News
you hear of him, is, that he is full of Curfing
And truly thus changeable are we all here. O
how suddenly many times do we change and fall
from the best into the worst of Frames and Carriages before God ? From Love to Hatred, from
Faith to Unbelief, from Holy Fear to Carnal Security, from Obedience to Rebellion, from Delight
in God to a Neglect of God, and a Weariness
of his Ways and Presence ? O let us be humbled
for this our exceeding Changeableness, and therein
our Unlikeness to God in his Unchangeableness.

2. Is God unchangeable ? Then how should we
be humbled that we do so often wrong God, char-
ing him with Unconstancy and Change, as we do ?
Such, my Beloved, is the Enmity and Unbelief of
our Hearts, that we are apt, upon all Occasions, to
take up hard Thoughts of God, and bring in black
Charges against him: Now we charge him with

Weaknefs, and anon with Folly, now with Un-
faithfulnefs, and anon with Unjuftice; now with
Cruelty, and anon with Change, which is a great
Evil, and calls for great Humbling · God is unchangeable, and he ftands much upon the Glory
of his Unchangeablenefs, and yet we charge him
with Change : What an Affront is this? This the
Pfalmift, whoever he was, came near unto, *Pfal.*
77. 7, 8, 9. *Will the Lord caft off for ever? And will
he be favourable no more? Is his Mercy clean gone for
ever? Doth his Promife fail for evermore? Hath God
forgotten to be Gracious? Hath he in Anger fhut up
his tender Mercies?* What is all this but in Effect
a Charging of God with Change? He is here even
upon the Point of concluding, that God is not the
God he was, that he is not fo Merciful, nor fo
Faithful, nor fo Gracious, as formerly he was. 'Tis
as if he fhould have faid, God was a God of Mercy, Mercy pleafed him, but now his Mercy is at
an end, and he is become all Severity;—he was
Faithful in his Promifes, but now his Promifes fail,
and fail utterly, he was a Gracious God, Grace
was his darling Attribute, but now his Grace is
forgotten by him : Thus for a time he did charge
God with change, though afterwards, as the Context tells us, his Faith recover'd it felf, and he
came to right Thoughts of God again. *Job* alfo
was deeply involved in this Guilt, *Job* 30. 21.
Thou art turned to be cruel to me, (fays he to God)
*thou wert a Kind, but now thou art a Cruel, God
to me.* The Church alfo is full of this, *Ifa.* 49. 14.
and fhe fpeaks it out, *Sion faid, the Lord hath for-
faken me, and my God hath forgotten me,* q. d. God
is changed, he is not the God he was. Thus I fay,
though God be unchangeable, yet we are apt to
charge him with Change, we are apt to think that
he is neither what he was, nor where he was; that
he is either not fo Good as he was, or elfe not fo

D 3   Great,

Great, so Powerful, so Wise, so Holy, so Faithful, so Gracious, as he was, and the like   *Behold*,
(says the Prophet) *the Lord's Hand is not shortned,
that it cannot save ; neither is his Ear heavy, that
it cannot hear, Isa. 59. 1.* They thought and concluded that God's Hand was shortned, that is, that
his Power was lessened, and that he was not as
able to save us now as formerly , they thought
and concluded that his Ear was grown heavy, that
is, that he was not so good, and kind, and ready,
to hear their Prayers now as formerly ; he was
a God able to save, but now, say they, he is not,
he was a Prayer-hearing God, but now, say they,
he is not : Thus they were ready to charge him
with Change : But, says the Prophet, there is no
such Matter, God is what he was, his Power is
the same, and his Readiness to hear, and help,
and save, is the same that ever it was.   There are,
among others, Two Cases especially in which we
are apt to charge the unchangeable God with
Change , one is, when we change in our Carriages
and Behaviour towards God ; the other is, when
God's Carriages and Dispensations are changed towards us , for indeed we are apt to measure God,
and judge of him, by his outward Carriage and Dispensations towards us , and when they are changed, we conclude he is changed : In *Gen.* 31 2.
'tis said, *that* Jacob *beheld the Countenance of* Laban,
and behold, it was not toward him as before : So we
many times behold the Countenance of God, his
outward Carriage and Dispensation towards us, and
'tis not towards us as before, his Countenance is
chang'd , and because his Countenance is not, we
think his Heart is not toward us as formerly, but
is changed.   O, my Beloved, let us take heed of
this grand Evil, of charging God with Change , 'tis
indeed a grand Evil, 'tis what is very grievous and
provoking to God, and 'tis what lays the Soul un-

der much deep dyed Guilt, 'tis indeed to rob God of
one of the Brighteft Jewels in his Crown; yea, 'tis to
un-God him For if he be changeab'e, he is not
God, tremble therefore, Reader, and tremble, O my
Soul, at the Thoughts of fuch a thing as this, namely, to charge the Unchangeable One with Change.

Is God unchangeable ? Then how fhould we be
humbled that we live fo much upon the Creature,
and fo little upon God ; fo much upon the Creature that does change, and fo little upon God that
changes not ? If we reflect ferioufly upon our
felves, we fhall find, (at leaft many of us) that
we live more upon the Creature, than we do upon God ; more upon broken Cifterns, than we do upon this Fountain of Living Waters ; at leaft, the
Beft and Holieft of us will find that we live too
much upon the Creature, and too little upon God;
witnefs the Eagernefs, Strength, and Vehemency,
of our Defires after the Creature more than after
God, and Communion with God: Alas ! how paf-
fionately many times do we long, and how vigo-
roufly do we purfue, after the Creature, when we
can be content well enough without God, and
Communion with God ? Witnefs the Frequency
of our Thoughts and Contemplations of and about
the Creature, more than of God, and about God.
Alas! *we mind Earthly Things*, as thofe did, *Phil.*
3 19. but how feldom do we think of God, and
contemplate God? Now that which is moft in our
Thoughts, that we live moft upon, witnefs our
Delight and Complacency in the Creature, more
than in God ? O, what Frefh, Springing, Vigo-
rous, 'Delights have we many times in the Creature ? But when, and how little, do we delight
our felves in God ? Now that which we take moft
Delight and Complacency in, that do we live moft
upon. Witnefs our Immoderate Griefs, and the
Bitternefs of Spirit we are ufually in for the Lofs

or Withdrawment of the Creatures, more than for
the Loss and Withdrawment of God and his Presence from us. Let this, or the other Creature-
Comfort, be withdrawn from us, and how do we
take on usually? And what Bitterness of Soul are
we filled withal? Then with *Hagar we lift up our
Voice and weep, Gen.* 21. 19. How did *Jonah,* that
Good Man, take on when the Gourd was withered?
Jon. 4. 7, 8, 9. But how seldom do we grieve,
and bleed, and mourn, for want of Communion
with God? Yea, how indifferent for the most
part are we whether we have Communion with
God or no? And what does this argue, but that
we live too much upon the Creature, and too little upon God? Thus if we seriously reflect upon
our selves, we shall find by these, and such like
things as these, that we live more upon the Creatures than we do upon God; and O how humbling shou'd this be upon us! The Creatures they
are vain, fading, changeable, Things, they are
even Vanity it self, and Changeableness it self,
but God is an Eternal, Unchangeable, Good, He
is the same for ever, an Unchangeable Fountain
of all Goodness, Sweetness, Blessedness, and Delight: Now to live upon these changeable Creatures, and not upon this unchangeable God, this
is a great Evil, and calls for great Mourning and
Humbling at our Hands. 'Tis a great Speech which
I have read in *Austin,* wherein he bewails this very Sin; *He that made me is Good,* (says he) *and he
is my Good, but in this I sinned, that not in Him,
but in his Creatures, I sought my self, and my other
Pleasures ;* that is, I took up my Solace and Happiness in the Creatures, and not in God; and what
then? *And so,* says he, *I ran my self upon many Dolors, Errors, and Confusion of Soul* And may not
many of us make the very same Complaint? He
that made us is Good, and he is our Good, but in
                                                      this

this we have finned, and do fin, that we live upon the Creatures, and not upon Him, and fo run our felves upon many Dolors, Errors, and Confufion of Soul : We live upon changeable Creatures more than upon an unchangeable God ; and hereby God is difhonoured, his Spirit is grieved, our Souls are bereaved of Good, yea, the beft Good, the Good of Grace, and Divine Difcoveries and Communications ; hereby we eat Husks, when we might eat Bread ; and we drink Swill, when we might drink Wine in our Father's Houfe. Hereby we are expofed to Sorrows, Snares, and Death ; yea, and hereby we are in Danger of being excluded from God for ever. Oh, my Beloved, let us be convinced of this Evil, and mourn over it : For my own part, when I reflect upon my felf, I find Caufe to fear that I have lived upon Creatures all my Days, upon changeable Creatures, to the great, if not total, Neglect of the unchangeable God ; and believe it, 'tis an hard thing to come off from the one, to live fo purely and intirely upon the other, as we ought to do : The Lord humble us for thefe Things.

CHAP. VIII.

God has a Revenue of Honour due to him upon the Account of his Unchangeablenefs. We fhould give him that Honour. Several fhort and plain Directions in order thereunto.

Every Attribute or Perfection of God, has a Revenue of Honour and Glory due to it from the Creature ; and 'tis a great Part of both the Wifdom and Duty of the Creature, to give to each

Attribute

Attribute and Perfection of his its proper Glory.
God is pleased to reveal and discover himself,
sometimes in one, and sometimes in another, Attribute of his; sometimes he reveals and discovers
himself in his Wisdom, sometimes in his Power,
sometimes in his Holiness, sometimes in his Faithfulness, sometimes in his Justice, sometimes in his
Grace, sometimes in his Greatness, and sometimes,
as here, in his Unchangeableness, now, I say, a
great Part of a Christian's Skill and Duty lyes in
this, To give to each Attribute, in which God reveals himself, its proper Glory, that is to say, to
honour God suitable to the present Revelation he
makes of himself. Now God being unchangeable,
our Work and Care should be, to give him the
Glory of his Unchangeableness, which, let me tell
you, is very dear to him. But how may we give
God the Glory due to this Attribute of his? Take
only these few plain Directions as to that briefly.

1. Would we give God the Glory of his Unchangeableness? Then let us get our Hearts deeply affected with this Attribute of his, being in an
Holy Manner over-awed therewith. The Unchangeableness of God is an awful Attribute, an
Attribute that challenges much Holy Awe and
Dread from the Creature; and when our Hearts
are indeed in an Holy Manner over-awed with the
Sense of this Attribute, and we are filled with a
reverential Regard of *God*, as he is an unchangea
ble God, then do we give him the Glory thereof:
This seems to be pointed at, *Isa.* 41. 4, 5. in *Verf.*
4. God reveals himself in his Unchangeableness,
when he says, *I the Lord, the First and the Last,
I am the First, and the Last* ; or, (as some render
it) I the same, I the same. And in *Verf* 5. you
have the Isles affected and over awed with this Attribute of his, *The Isles saw it, and feared :* Accor
dingly, if we would indeed give God the Glory

of

of his Unchangeableneſs, we ſhould labour to get our Hearts over-awed with the Senſe and Apprehenſion thereof, we ſhould dwell much in the Meditation of this Perfection of God, our Language ſhould be, Well, how changeable ſoever we are, yet God is unchangeable, he is for ever the ſame, unchangeable in Greatneſs, unchangeable in Goodneſs, unchangeable in Wiſdom, unchangeable in Power, unchangeable in Holineſs, unchangeable in Faithfulneſs, unchangeable in Fulneſs and Sufficiency, he is every way an unchangeable God; what he was, he is, what he is, he will be for ever : Thus we ſhould ſit down and contemplate this Attribute, till we find our Hearts affected and over awed by it.

2. Would we give God the Glory of his Unchangeableneſs? Then let us aſcribe this Attribute to God, and celebrate his Glory in it. In *Deut.* 32. 3. we are called upon *to aſcribe Greatneſs to God* ; and as we ſhould aſcribe Greatneſs, ſo we muſt aſcribe Unchangeableneſs, to God, and withal admire and adore him therein, if we mean to give him the Glory of this Attribute of his : This the *Pſalmiſt* does once and again, *From everlaſting* (ſays he) *to everlaſting thou art God*, Pſal. 90 1, 2. and again, *They ſhall periſh*, (ſays he, ſpeaking of the Heavens) *but thou Lord ſhalt endure ; they ſhall be changed, but thou art the ſame, and thy Years ſhall have no end*, *Pſal.* 102. 25, 26, 27. He celebrates the Glory of God in his Unchangeableneſs, admiring and adoring him in this Perfection of his: The Church does the ſame thing in *Rev* 4 8. where we read of *Four Beaſts which reſt not Day and Night, ſaying, Holy, Holy, Holy, Lord God Almighty, which was, and is, and is to come :* Pray mark, Firſt, They celebrate the Glory of God's Holineſs, ſaying, *Holy, Holy, Holy.* Secondly, They celebrate

the

the Glory of God's Power and Sovereignty, *Lord God Almighty* · Thirdly, They celebrate the Glory of God's Unchangeableness and Eternity, *which was, which is, and which is to come*, *q. d.* Thou art an Holy God, and we adore thee for thine Holiness; thou art a Potent and Sovereign Lord, and we adore thee for thy Power and Sovereignty, thou art an Unchangeable *God*, and we adore thee for thine Unchangeableness; how fading foever the Creatures are, thou art still the same. In like manner should we do, we should afcribe Unchangeableness to God, and be much in admiring and adoring him for, and in, this Perfection of his, this is all that we can do, and 'tis indeed our glorifying of him, to difplay and make mention of the Excellencies and Perfections of God, and with both our Spirits and Tongues to celebrate the Glory of them, which indeed will be our Work for ever; O let us be much in it now.

3. Would we give God the Glory of his Unchangeableness? Then let us fee and acknowledge him and his Unchangeableness to be the fole Spring and Fountain of all that Unchangeableness that either Men or Angels do attain unto; the Creatures, Men and Angels not excepted, in themfelves are all changeable, but yet there is a Blefied Unchangeableness, which fome of them, I mean the Saints and Holy Angels, do at laft attain unto, they are (as the School-men fpeak of them) *in omni bono confirmati*, eternally and unchangeably confirmed in all Good, in all Holinefs, all Happinefs, and whence comes this to pafs? Verily, from the Unchangeablenefs of God, that is the Spring and Fountain of all. Were not God unchangeable, unchangeable in his Covenant, Counfel, and Love, they would never arrive to fuch an Unchangeablenefs, to God's Unchangeablenefs therefore we should give the Glory of it. Look

as Chriſt ſaid in another Caſe, *Becauſe I live, ye ſhall live alſo,* *Joh.* 14. 19. So may God ſay, both to Men and Angels, becauſe I am unchangeable, therefore ſhall ye be unchangeable alſo : Indeed, the Unchangeableneſs which Saints and Angels do attain unto, is but a Beam, as it were, of God's Unchangeableneſs, emitted down upon them, they ſhall be unchangeably holy, becauſe God is ſo ; they are unchangeably bleſſed, becauſe God is ſo ; and they have Communion with him by Chriſt in his unchangeable Holineſs and Bleſſedneſs, ſee therefore, and acknowledge God and his Un-changeableneſs in that Unchangeableneſs which Saints and Angels attain unto, aſcribing theirs wholly to his.

4. Would we give God the Glory of his Un-changeableneſs? Then let us live upon this Un-changeableneſs of his: The more we live upon the Unchangeableneſs of God, the more we ho-nour it, and give him the Glory of it: Now we ſhould live upon it under a double Notion.———

1. We ſhould live upon it as the ſole Cauſe of all our Preſervation, expecting all from it, and aſcri-bing all to it, this God challenges from us in the very Text ; *I am the Lord, I change not, therefore ye are not conſumed* ; *q. d.* 'Tis from my Unchangea-bleneſs that you are alive, that you are out of Hell, and 'tis my Unchangeableneſs that muſt keep you alive, and preſerve you for ever, and I expect you ſhould own it, and live upon it, accordingly· Our Language ſhould be, I am alive, and why? Be-cauſe God is unchangeable, I am out of Hell, and why? Becauſe God is unchangeable, yea, I hope I ſhall live, and that for ever, but why? Becauſe God is unchangeable True, I am a changeable Creature, and being left to my ſelf, I ſhall quickly forfeit Life, Soul, Salvation, and all, yea, I am forfeiting all every Day and Hour by Sin ; but God

is

is an unchangeable God, he is for ever the same, his Counsel, his Covenant, his Love, are all un-changeable, and therefore I do live, and shall live, yea, live eternally: Oh, this is so to live upon the Unchangeableness of God, as to give him the Glory of that Perfection of his.——— 2. We should live upon the Unchangeableness of God as a Sweet Spring of Comfort and Refreshment to us under all those afflictive Changes, which here in this World we meet withal: We here meet with many affli-ctive Changes; *Changes and War are upon us*; but the Unchangeableness of God is a Sweet Spring of Comfort and Refreshment in all, and under all; and when we live upon it as such, bearing up our Souls thereupon, then do we give this Attribute its proper Glory. This is what is called for, *Isa.* 26. 4. *Trust ye in the Lord for ever*, (that is, live, rest, depend, upon him: Why so?) *for in the Lord Jehovah is everlasting Strength*, the Words are, the Rock of Ages, the Rock of this Age, the Rock of former Ages, the Rock of Ages to come, a Rock in all Ages, and the Rock of all Ages, that is to say, a firm, unchangeable, One; and being such an One, he is, he must be, the proper Ob-ject of Trust, and unless we do trust in him, and live upon him, as our Life, we do not give him his proper Glory: We should, as it were, sit down, and say, Well, though my Estate changes, yet God does not change, and so long all is well: Tho' my Friends and Comforts change, my Friends turn Enemies, and my Comforts Crosses, yet God does not change, and so long all is well: Yea, 'tis true, my Spirit changes, there is no Fixedness, no Stability, in it, as to any thing that is good and gracious; yet however God changes not, he is al-ways the same, and I'll live on him; *The Lord lives, and blessed be my Rock*, (says *David*) Psal. 18. 46. Friends die, Trade dies, and my self am

á dying, but *the Lord lives*, and there is enough in
that to bear me up under all: O when thus we
live upon God's Unchangeablenefs, as a Spring and
Fountain of Comfort to us under all afflictive
Changes here, then do we give him the Glory of
this Attribute of his.

5. Would we give God the Glory of his Unchangeablenefs? Then let us labour to imitate him,
and to be as like him herein as poffibly we can ; let
us labour, as much as poffible, for an Holy Unchangeablenefs, a Fixednefs and Stability in what is good,
even here, and that in Conformity to God : We
caft an Honour (as one obferves) upon them whom
we imitate; for by our Imitation of them we acknowledge an Excellency in them, which is all
that honouring in the firft Notion of it imports;
fure I am, the more like to God we covet to be,
and the more we imitate him in this Perfection of
his, by coming up to an Holy Evennefs and Stability in what is Good, the more do we honour him,
and give him his proper Glory : But this may poffibly be fpoken to in a Chapter by it felf in its proper Place. Thus you fee how to give God that
Glory which is due to him upon the Account of
his Unchangeablenefs.

CHAP. IX.

*God's Unchangeablenefs fhould induce us to chufe him
for our God and Portion, and to take up the Reft
and Happinefs of our Souls in him, with Arguments
to quicken thereunto.*

THE Unchangeablenefs of God calls aloud upon us all to chufe him for our God and Portion, and to take up the Reft and Happinefs of our
Soul's in him, and not in the Creatures. The
Truth is, to chufe God for our God and Portion,
and

and to take up our Reſt and Happineſs in him, is
what every Diſcovery of God, in one or another
Excellency or Perfeċtion of his, does challenge
and call for at our Hands. Does he reveal himſelf
to be an Holy God ? This calls upon us to chuſe
him for our God and Portion, and to get an Intereſt in his Holineſs Does God reveal himſelf to
be a Gracious God, a God of Grace and Love?
This calls upon us to chuſe him for our God and
Portion, and to get an Intereſt in his Love: Doth
he reveal himſelt to be a Faithful God, a God that
keepeth Covenant and Mercy ? This calls upon us
to chuſe him for our God and Portion, and;to get
an Intereſt in his Faithfulneſs: So here: Does
God reveal himſelf to be an Unchangeable God ?
This calls upon us to chuſe him for our God and
Portion, and to get an Intereſt in his Unchangeableneſs, taking up the Reſt and Happineſs of our
Souls in him ; and accordingly, O that we would
look and live above changeable Creatures, taking
up our Reſt and Happineſs in this vnchangeable
God, which to do is even infinitely our ſafeſt and
ſweeteſt Courſe. For pray conſider, who or what
you will chuſe for your Portion, and wherein will
you place the Reſt and Happineſs of your Souls, if
not in the unchangeable God ? Sure I am, you
have but God or the Creature to make Choice of.
Now what is the Creature to God ? What is the
changeable Creature to the unchangeable God?
Alas! the one is infinitely ſhort of the other : God
indeed is every way, and in all reſpeċts, a moſt
deſirable Good , he is an original Good, a full
Good, a ſuitable Good, a ſatisfying Good, an unmixed Good, an all-ſufficient Good, and, which
crowns all, an unchangeable Good, a Good that
never fades, never fail-. *He is the Living God,
and ſtedfaſt for ever, Dan. 6. 26.* The Creatures are
all changeable and periſhing. An Heathen could
ſay, |

ſay, *We live among periſhing things :* And 'twas a great Saying of one of the Ancients, *We have nothing here* (ſays he) *of any long Continuance; and all the Felicity of this World is gone while we hold it, and loſt even while we enjoy it ;* ſuch, and ſo great, is the Changeableneſs and Uncertainty of all theſe Things: But God (as you have heard) and all that Good that is in him, is always and for ever the ſame, which ſpeaks him to be Infinitely ſweet and deſirable, and ſo Infinitely worthy to be embraced by us for our God and Portion: This indeed crowns and perfects all that Good that is in God. Look, as the Changeableneſs of the Creatures lowers and allays that Good and Sweetneſs that is in them, ſo the Unchangeableneſs of God does infinitely raiſe and commend that Good and Excellency that is in him. Had the Creatures Ten Thouſand times more Good and Excellency in them than they have, yet this one Conſideration, that they are changeable, were enough to damp all, and quaſh all ; though the Creatures had never ſo much Sweetneſs and Goodneſs in them, and though I had never ſo full, free, and ample, Injoyment of them, though the Streams ran never ſo pleaſantly on each Hand of me, yet this one Thought, that all this is fading and changeable, and will laſt but for a Seaſon, were enough to allay my Joy, and even imbitter all to me. So on the other Hand, though God be ſuch an Infinite Ocean of Goodneſs, Sweetneſs, and Bleſſedneſs, as he is, yet that which crowns all, is his Unchangeableneſs in all , and without this 'tis not the Whole of God could make us Happy. Now ſhall the Conſideration hereof induce you to chuſe him for your God and Portion, and take up your Reſt and Happineſs in him for ever ? Poſſibly you have never yet choſen God to be your God and Portion, nor have you taken up the Reſt and Happineſs of your

Souls in him, you have chosen the Creatures, you have chosen this World, you have chosen carnal, sensual, things, and in these have you placed your Rest and Happiness, but as for God, he has hitherto been *far from your Reins*, you have centred in changeable Creatures, and forgotten the unchangeable God. But will you now change your Choice, and take up a new Rest? Oh now let an unchangeable God, not changeable Creatures, be your God and Portion, your Rest and Happiness. O that the Language of your Souls to God might now be that of the *Psalmist*, Psal. 73. 25. *Whom have I in Heaven but thee? And there is none upon Earth that I desire besides thee.* Lord, thou, and thou alone, shall be my God, my Rest, my Portion, my Happiness, and my All, for ever. Indeed I had chosen the Creatures for my Portion and Happiness, but now I renounce that Choice, I'll have no more to do with changeable Creatures; the World was my Happiness, and I sat down with it, *so foolish was I, and ignorant*, but now I have done with the World, this flitting, fading, dying, World, and thou Lord alone shall be my All for ever: Oh that you would indeed thus chuse the unchangeable God, and take up your Rest and Happiness in him this Day: And you that have chosen him, and taken up your Happiness in him, make a new Choice of him, and take up your Rest more purely and entirely in him, say over this unchangeable One, *This God is our God for ever and ever*, Psal. 48. 14. Oh, labour to get more above the Creatures, and live more in God, and upon God. The more purely and entirely you take up your Rest in God, the sweeter will he be to you, and the more Satisfaction will your Souls find in him. Now to quicken you thus to chuse God, and live upon him and his Unchangeableness.

1. Con-

1. Confider what a changeable World we live in, we live in a changeable World, in a World that rings Changes every Day, many Changes and great Changes; the Truth is, This World is a very changeable World, and 'tis not long e'er it will be changed once for all, the Day is coming when *all thefe things fhall be diffolved, the Heavens fhall pafs away with a Noife, the Earth fhall melt with fervent Heat,* 2 *Pet* 3. 10, 11. and in the mean time the World is not with ut its Changes, and how great Changes we may live to fee who knows? Such Changes feem to be coming upon the World, as that nothing but an unchangeable God will be able to bear us up under them In *Luke* 21. 25, 26 we read of *Difrefs of Nations which fhall be upon the Earth with Perplexity, Mens Hearts failing them for fear, and for looking after thofe things that fhall come to pafs upon the Euth* · The Sum of which amounts to this, that there fhall be fuch Changes, fuch Rendings, fuch Shakings, fuch Terrible Convulfions and Concuffions, wrought in the Nations of the World, fuch Defolations fhall be made, and fuch Terrible Storms of Wrath and Vengeance fhall fall upon the World, as that Men fhall be even exanimated, and driven to their Wits End, they fhall fall under a *Deliquium Animi,* a Swooning of Spirit, they fhall breathe out their very Souls, or, they fhall be filled with fuch Anguifh, Horror, and Confufion, of Soul, as that they fhall be ready to lay violent Hands upon themfelves, and take away their own Lives: And, my Beloved, fhould we live to fee fuch things, how good will an unchangeable God be? O, Sirs! living in fuch a changeable World, who would not fix upon an unchangeable God, as a Man's Portion and Happinefs? Who would not get upon, yea, into, this *Rock of Ages?* And how good, how fweet, will it

be

be to have an unchangeable God to retreat to, and ark in?

2. Confider what changeable things all our Creature-Comforts and Contentments are: As the World wherein we live is a changeable World, fo all our Creature-Comforts are changeable Comforts, should the World ftand where it does, and as it does, without any fuch Changes as we have mentioned, yet our beft Creature-Comforts here are fubject to change every Day, and how foon we may fay of one or another, or all of them, as *Jacob* fometimes did of his Two Sons, *Jofeph* and *Simeon, Gen.* 42. 36. Jofeph *is not, and* Simeon *is not.* How foon we may fay, this and that Comfort is not, who can tell? I have now a Trade, to morrow, it may be, I fhall have none. I have now an Eftate, to morrow, it may be, I fhall have none. I have now a pleafant Habitation, to morrow, it may be, it will be in Afhes. I have now my Friends and Relations about me, my Husband, or my Wife, lying pleafantly in my Bofom; my Children like Olive branches round about my Table, to morrow, it may be, they will all fleep in the Duft, and go down to the Gates of the Grave, and I fhall fee them no more. Alas! thefe things *are not,* (as *Solomon* fpeaks of Riches) fuch is their Changeablenefs, that they have fcarce a Being, or, fuppofe thefe things fhould ftay with us, yet how foon may they be imbitter'd to us? How foon may the beft of this Wine be turned into Wormwood? How foon may the fweeteft of thefe Comforts be changed into bitter Croffes? Sometimes *the Defire of our Eyes is taken away from us with a Stroke,* (as God threatned the Prophet of old) that is, fuddenly, and e'er ever we are aware of it, our deareft, fweeteft, and moft delightful, Comforts are taken from us. At other times the Defire of our Eyes becomes the Burthen of our

Souls,

Souls, our deareſt Comforts are inbittered to us; that which Yeſterday was ſweet and pleaſant, to Day poſſibly is bitter and burthenſome to us, that which to Day is the Joy of our Hearts, to Morrow, it may be, will be as a Goad in our Sides, and as Thorns in our Eyes : O how ſoon many times do our moſt pleaſant Streams turn into Waters of *Marah* to us ! Now all on this Side God being thus changeable, who would not reſt in him and his Unchangeableneſs ? Oh Unchangeableneſs ! Unchangeableneſs ! This is to be found in God alone, and therefore let him alone be the Reſt and Portion of our Souls.

3. Conſider how near our laſt and great Change is unto us. Should the World never wax old, nor admit of any Change, and ſhould our Creature-Comforts and Contentments live and laſt for ever, yet we our ſelves muſt change, we are fading, dying, periſhing, Creatures, we paſs under many Changes, and great Changes, and 'tis but a little while e'er our laſt and great Change will come. Death is our laſt and great Change till the Reſurrection So the Holy Ghoſt by *Job* ſpeaks of it, *Job* 14 14. and this is a great Change indeed, a Change from Work to Reward, from Time to Eternity, a Change out of this World into another; from theſe Tabernacles of Clay, to live in eternal Regions, either of Light or Darkneſs, and thus ſhall we all be changed· A few Years, a few Months, a few Weeks, a few Days, a few Hours, yea, it may be, but a few Moments, more, and we ſhall all be thus changed, changed by Death out of Time into Eternity, and how much then are we concerned to make Choice of, and take up our Reſt in, an unchangeable God ? Then, namely, when we paſs under this Change, to be ſure nothing but Unchangeableneſs will be of any Avail to us, and this is to be found in God alone. him

therefore

therefore fhould we chufe and take up our Reft in.
This very Confideration induced *David* to make a
frefh Choice of God, and cleave more entirely to
him, as his Reft and Happinefs, *Pf.* 39. 5,6,7 *Behold,*
O Lord, thou haft made my Days as an Hand-breadth,
and mine Age is as nothing before thee : Verily, every
Man at his beft Eftate is altogether Vanity , furely
every Man walketh in a vain Shew, furely they are dif-
quieted in vain Well, and what now ? Why, fays
he, *And now, Lord, what wait I for ? My Hope is*
in thee. He faw his Vanity and Changeablenefs, as
alfo the Vanity and Changeablenefs of all others,
both Perfons and Things ; he faw both himfelf
and all others in their very beft State to be not only vain, but even Vanity it felf, fubject to Change
every Hour , in the Sight and Senfe of which he
cleaves to God, chufes him, centers in him, as his
God, his Portion, his All: *Now, Lord, what wait*
I for ? My Hope is in thee , q. d. Now, Lord, that
I have feen my own Vanity and Changeablenefs,
and the Vanity and Changeablenefs of others too,
now I look to thee, I cleave to thee, I reft in thee,
as my only Good, Portion, and Happinefs I
have now done with the Streams, with the Creatures, and Creature-Contentments, and I'll now
bathe only in the Fountain, reft wholly in thy felf,
the Fountain of Living Waters. And, my Beloved,
did we dwell more in the Confideration of the
Nearnefs of our laft and great Change, we fhould
doubtlefs cleave more clofely and entirely to the
unchangeable God, as our Reft and Portion: Our
thus *numbering our Days,* deep and frequent Confi
deration of the Shortnefs of our Lives, and how
foon we may be changed, would make us to *apply*
our Hearts to this Wifdom, to get an Intereft in the
Unchangeable God, *Pfal.* 90. 12. O be much
therefore in this Work.

4. Confider,

4. Confider that then, and not till then, fhall we be Happy indeed, when we come to look and live above changeable Creatures upon an unchangeable God. 'Tis Happinefs, my Beloved, that is the great Intereft of Souls, and 'tis Happinefs we all defire and purfue after, now then are we Happy indeed, and not till then, when we get above the Creatures, and take up our Reft in the unchangeable God. Pray, Sirs, let us confider things a little; fuppofe you had this whole World at Will, and might enjoy as much of the Creature as your Souls could wifh ; fuppofe you could all your Days live in a Paradife of all earthly Delights, and fwim chin-deep in the Streams of all Creature-Contentments, yet what were all this? Alas! it would not make up one Dram of true Happinefs; your Happinefs muft be in God ftill. Mind how the *Pfalmift* fpeaks as to this, *Pfal.* 144. 15. *Happy is the People that is in fuch a Cafe; yea, Happy is that People whofe God is the Lord.* In what Cafe was this? Why, a Cafe of outward Profperity, a Cafe of enjoying an Affluence of all outward Creature-Contentments; for of thefe he had fpoken before. But, *David,* is this really your Judgment? And do you give it us for a Divine Truth, that thefe things make Men Happy? No, (fays he) I rather herein tell you what the World's Judgments is, and wherein they look upon Happinefs to confift; they think thofe of all others to be the Happieft People, who enjoy moft of this World, moft Eafe, moft Pleafure, moft of Creature-Comforts. But (fays he) I am of another Mind, I account them the Happy People who have the Lord for their God, that is, who have a Covenant-Relation to, and Intereft in, the Bleffed God, 'tis God, not the Creature, the Enjoyment of whom makes Happy. The former Propofition [*Happy is the People that is in fuch a Cafe*] fhews what carnal Men judge

concerning

concerning Happiness, and what makes Happy in
their Account, the latter Proposition, [yea, *Hap-*
py is the People whose God is the Lord] shews what
true Happiness indeed is, and wherein it consists,
which is in an Interest in God, in the unchangeable One. Or, *this latter is* (as one observes) *a*
Correction of the former ; *and 'tis as if he should say,*
but I would rather say, they are the Happy Souls who
have the true God, not the changeable Creature propi-
tious to them. Oh, 'tis not the Creature, but God,
an Interest in, and Communion with, Unchangeableness that makes Happy : 'Tis the joint Language of all the Creatures, Happiness is not in us,
we are all Vanity, and subject to change, and cannot make eternal Souls Happy, Happiness lyes in
God alone, where alone both Fulness and Unchangeableness, Sufficiency and Immutability, are
to be found. To look for Happiness in the Creature, is to seek the Living among the Dead ; but
to look for it in God, that is, to seek it at the
Fountain-head of all true Happiness. What shall
I say? God is his own Happiness, he is eternally
Blessed in and with himself, (as has been before
declared) and he is the Happiness of his Creatures,
both Saints and Angels, and when God makes his
People, his Saints and Servants, perfectly Happy,
which he never does till he takes them to Heaven,
he then takes them from all their Creature-Content
ments, and he admits and receives them into the
full and single Enjoyment of himself. 'Twere easie
to shew that nothing short of God and his Un
changeableness can possibly make Happy, and ac
cordingly that we shall never be Happy indeed,
till we learn to carry our Happiness above the Road
of Creatures, and place it wholly and intirely in
God. But I must not run out too far here. Oh,
my Beloved, that Man is certainly Happ est whose
Heart and Life are Holiest, and whose Communion

mon with God is fulleft; he that enjoys moft of God, whether he enjoys much or little of the Creature, he it is that is moft Happy. 'Tis a great Saying which I have read in *Auftin,* fpeaking to thofe that feek Happinefs in the Creature, *Seek what you feek,* (fays he) that is, feek Happinefs, *but know that 'tis not to be found where you feek it; you feek a Bleffed Life in the Region of Death, but 'tis not to be found there, for how fhould there be a Bleffed Life found, where there is not fo much as Life found?* And elfewhere, fpeaking to God, *All things are full of Trouble and Difficulty, and thou alone art Reft and Happinefs,* (fays he.) Truly the Creature (as *Solomon* tells us) is nothing elfe but *Vanity and Vexation of Spirit;* but in God there is Reft, there is Happinefs, there is Satisfaction of Soul, to be found; and if you would be Happy indeed, chufe him, and place your Reft and Happinefs in him alone.

5. Confider that God freely offers himfelf, as an unchangeable Good, in his Covenant to you. You know how he fpeaks to Sinners, even to Sinners, *Ifa.* 55. 3. *Come unto me, and I will make an Everlafting Covenant with you.* And pray what is this Covenant? Why, *I will be your God,* that, you know, is the grand Promife of it, *Jer.* 31. 33. In the Covenant God offers himfelf to Sinners in all his Glorious Excellencies and Perfections: His Language therein to them is, Come Souls, fee what a God I am, how Great, how Good, how Rich, how Glorious, fee what Treafures of Light and Life, of Love and Glory, there are in me; and lo! I am willing to be yours, your God, your Friend, your Father, your Portion, your Happinefs, your All, for ever: Look, whatever I am, that I will be to you; and whatever I can do, that I wi'l do for you. Thus he offers himfelf in all his Glorious Excellencies and Perfections to you, and as in all,

E

fo

so particularly in his Unchangeableness, Come, says he, *I am the Lord, I change not*, and as such an one do I tender my self to you; my Unchangeableness shall be the Rock of your Rest, the Immutability of my Nature, my Counsel, my Covenant, my Love, is a sure footing for your Faith, and a firm Foundation for your Comfort. While I am I will be Life and Blessedness to you, I'll be a never failing Fountain of Peace, Joy, and Satisfaction, to you, *I am the First and the Last, he who was, and is, and is to come*; and as such I will be yours for ever, and when the World, and all that is therein, shall be burnt up, I will be a standing Portion for you; when the whole World is like a tumbling Ocean round about you, I'll be a *Rock of Ages* to you, and be not afraid of me, I am a God of Grace and Love: 'Tis true, I am *the Great and High God*, but my Highness shall stoop, and my Greatness shall condescend, to you; yea, and nothing shall stand between you and me, no Sin, no Vileness, no Unworthiness, of yours, I know you are poor, vile, sinful, worthless, Worms, infinitely unworthy of me, I know your Sins are many, and the Distance between me and you is great, but all this shall not hinder you from an Interest in Me and my Unchangeableness, if you will take hold of my Covenant, chuse me for your God and Portion, and take up the Rest and Happiness of your Souls in me. Thus God reveals and offers himself in his Covenant to us; and does he thus offer himself in his Covenant to us, and shall we not chuse him for our God and Portion? Shall we stick in the Creature still, and reject the Offer God makes of himself to us? God forbid! Oh let us now chuse this unchangeable God, and let him be our Rest, our Portion, our Happiness, and our All, for ever. Let us reason Matters a little in our own Souls, the World that is full of Change

all my Creature-Comforts and Contentments they
are fubject to change, I am not fure of them one
Moment, my own great and laft Change is near at
Hand, I know not how foon 'twill come upon me,
nothing but the unchangeable God can make me
Happy, and he freely offers himfelf in his Covenant to me, and fhall I yet, notwithftanding all
this, neglect him? Shall I cleave to the Creature,
and not to this unchangeable God? By no means,
He, not the fading, dying, Creature, fhall be my
Portion and my Happinefs for ever. Or, if all this
does not do, then once more,

6. Confider, how fad and dreadful a thing it
will be to have the Unchangeablenefs of God
againft you. This is a fure Rule, that unlefs we
make God ours by chufing of him, and clofing in
his Covenant with him, as our God and Portion,
he and all his Attributes will at laft be found
againft us, againft us to deftroy us, and make us
miferable for ever. If we make not God's Unchangeablenefs ours, and ingage it not for us, by
chufing him as Unchangeable, his Unchangeablenefs will ftand for ever engaged againft us, and
O! how fad will that be? 'Tis fad to have any Attribute of God againft a Man, but to have his Unchangeablenefs againft us, how fad is that? O for
a Man to have God for his eternal Enemy, God
eternally and unchangeably fet againft him, this is
enough to render him compleatly and unchangeably miferable. Again, therefore let me call upon
you to look and live above changeable Creatures,
and to chufe, reft in, and live upon, the unchangeable God, as your God and Portion, look
upon him in Chrift, in whom you will find him
infinitely full of Love and Sweetnefs, in whom you
will find him Love it felf. *God is Love,* 1 Joh. 4. 8.
and accordingly let your Souls chufe him, and
cleave to him, as yours for ever.

E 2 CHAP.

CHAP. X.

We are to imitate God, and labour for a Likeness to him in his Unchangeableness, by being more constant in that which is good; this, in some Measure, is attainable in this World, 'tis the Perfection of the Soul, where attained, and brings him near the Life of Heaven.

UNchangeableness being one of the Glorious Excellencies and Perfections of God, why should we not imitate him? Why should we not labour to be like unto him herein? Why should we not covet and press after an Holy Unchangeab'eness in our Spirits and Walkings with him? Sure I am, 'tis what his Unchangeableness calls upon us for. *From the Consideration of God's Immutability,* (says a Learned Man) *it follows that we also should labour to be immutable in the Things of God, in Faith, in Hope, in Love, and the like* Look as the Consideration of God's Holiness calls for Holiness in us, and the Consideration of his Goodness and Mercy calls for Goodness and Mercy in us, and the Consideration of his Patience calls for Patience in us, and the like; so the Consideration of his Unchangeableness calls for an Holy Unchangeableness, at least somewhat like it, an Holy Evenness, Steadiness, and Fixedness, of Spirit in our Ways and Walkings with him, and before him; it calls upon us to be more constant and uniform in all Holy Obedience, and in the Exercise of all Grace. True, my Beloved, there are some things so peculiarly appropriate to God, that in respect of them there can be no formal Likeness in the Creature to Him; and it would be Impious Boldness for any to aspire thereunto; such are his Supream Dominion and Sovereign Authority, his Absolute Independency

dency and Self sufficiency, &c. Now in thefe, while Men affect to imitate him, they (as one obferves) wickedly affront him. But now fome other Perfections there are found in the Bleffed God not fo incommunicable and appropriate to him, but that his Creatures may be faid to have fome Participation thereof with him, and fo far to be truly like him , fuch are his Holinefs, his Juftice, his Mercy, his Patience, and the like, wherein 'tis our Duty, as well as our Glory, to imitate him, and to labour for as great a Refemblance, and as full a Conformity, to him as poffibly we can. In *Mat.* 5. 48. Chrift commands us to *be perfect, as our Father which is in Heaven is perfect* ; and *Eph.* 5. 1. we are enjoyned *to be Followers of God, as Dear Children : Be ye Followers of God* ; the Word is, Be ye Imitators of God, be ye like to him, bearing his Image upon you , and if you are his Children inceed, you will do fo : We fhould imitate God in all his imitable Excellencies and Perfections ; yea, this obferve moreover, that where there cannot be a proper and formal Likenefs or Similitude in us to God, in Refpect of thofe peculiarly appropriate Excellencies that are in him, yet even there fhou'd we labour for Impreffions, Affections, Difpofions, and Demeanors, of Soul towards him, fuitable and anfwerable to thofe Excellencies and Perfections of his. As for Inftance, he being abfolutely Supream, there ought to be in us an humble Subjection and Self refignation of Soul, difpofing us to conftant Obedience to him So he being fimply and abfolutely independent and felf fufficient, there ought to be in us a Self emptinefs and Nothingnefs, living wholly and entirely out of our felves upon him as fuch a God, fetching all in from his Fountain-fulnefs· Thus where we are not capable of any formal Likenefs to God, we fhould yet ftudy his Perfections, and labour for Difpofi-

tions

tions of Spirit, and Demeanors of Soul suitable
thereunto, but where we are capable of any Likeness to him, there we should covet it, and press
after it God therefore being unchangeable, we
should labour for an Holy Unchangeableness in our
Spirits and Walkings before him, we should imitate him, and conform to him herein, so far as we
are capable of so doing, we should labour for
more Fixedness, more Evenness, more Constancy
and Uniformity, in all Grace and Holiness, in all
Heavenliness and Obedience, in all Acts of Duty and
Walking with God Tis what in a good Measure
may be attained unto even here in this World.
Tis possible, my Beloved, for these roving, in-
constant, unstable, Souls of ours, to be in some
good Measure brought up to an Holy Evenness
and Unchangeableness in the Ways and Things of
God, for this is what some of the Saints have attained unto. In *Gen.* 5. 22. 'tis said of *Enoch*, that
*he walked with God Three Hundred Years, and begat
Sons and Daughters* Of others 'tis said that they
begat such and such, and they lived so many Years
afterwards · But of *Enoch* 'tis said he *begat* Methu-
selah, *and walked with God Three Hundred Years*, as
if his whole Life for that Three Hundred Years
were one continued and uninterrupted Course of
walking with God. The Phrase (as a Learned
Critick observes) seems to carry this in it, *that he
had God so present always with him, and he so accom-
modated himself to the Pleasure of God, as that he
seemed perpetually to walk with him.* His Life was,
as it were, one constant Course and Series of walking with Him This also is what God calls for, *Be
stedfast, immoveable, always abounding in the Work of
the Lord,* 1 *Cor.* 15 58. This is what the Apostles
are ever and anon praying for, both for themselves and others. *The God of all Grace establish,
strengthen, settle, you,* 1 *Pet.* 5. 10. This is what
being

being attained is the Crown and Perfection of a
Christian, so in that same, 1 Pet. 5. 10. *The God
of all Grace, after you have suffered a while, make
you perfect, stablish, strengthen, you.* To be stablisht
and settled in our Spirits and Ways, in Holy
Things, this is our Perfection. 'Tis indeed the
Glory of Christianity, and the Honour of a Christian. Oh, my Beloved, the more even and uniform we are in the Things and Ways of God, the
more Excellent and Perfect we are, and the more
Amiable in the Sight of God. Oh, 'tis not the fil-
shy, high-flown, Talking, but the even and steady
Christian, that is most Excellent, most Amiable, in
God's Eye, this is a Crown of Glory indeed upon
the Head of a poor Soul. 'Twas Queen *Eliz zbeth*'s
Motto, *Semper eadem*, always the same, and truly
were it more in an Holy Respect the Christian's
Motto, he would be more Glorious than he is:
Rawlins you left me, and Rawlins you find me, said
that Martyr, meaning, that he was still in the
same Mind, the same Spirit, being constant to his
Testimony, which was his Crown and Glory. *'Tis
an High and Great Thing* (says one to his Friend)
*which thou desirest, and even borders upon a Deity,
it to be moved and changed.* Sure I am, 'tis an
high and Great Thing in Spirituals to come up to
an Holy Evenness and Fixedness of Soul, this is
that which Honours the Gospel, this is that which
renders Religion amiable, this is that which makes
way for full and constant Communion with God,
for abiding Consolations, this is that which delights the Heart of God, this is that which brings
us near to the State and Life of Heaven, for there
the Saints and Angels are fixed and unchangeably
confirmed in all Good, in all Holiness, in all Happiness. Oh, labour for as much of this Holy Unchangeableness as possibly may be attained unto here
on Earth, and then sigh and long for that Life and

State,

State, where you shall know no Change for ever, but be perfectly, unchangeably, and eternally, Holy and Happy, as God himself is, for *you shall be like him, and see him as he is,* 1 *Joh.* 3. 2. 'Tis true, 'tis no easie thing to fix our roving Spirits, and reduce them to a Steadiness in what is good, but remember, the God you are to have Recourse to, to do this great Work for you, is *the God of all Grace,* as you have it in the prequoted Place, 1 *Pet.* 5. 10. and he therefore can do it with Ease for you Oh, look to him for this great Blessing, this high Attainment.

CHAP. XI.

The Unchangeableness of God a Sweet Spring of Comfort to his People : Several Consolatory Conclusions thence.

AS God's Unchangeableness calls for much Duty from, so it ministers much sweet Comfort to his poor Church and People· The Truth is, there is scarce any such Spring and Treasury of Comfort as this is; *God's Immutability* (says one) *is the best Cordial to refresh a fainting Soul.* The great Cordial God sent *Israel* in their Distress was this, *I am that I am,* I am an unchangeable God, *Exod.* 3. 14. and indeed that was enough for them : But more particularly, there are several Consolatory Conclusions which flow from God's Unchangeableness, Conclusions which do carry strong Consolation in them.

1. God being unchangeable, his Glory shall live, and in due time shine forth conspicuously before all, for this see *Isa.* 42. 8. *I am the Lord, I am Jehovah, I am he who was, and is, and is to com*

come, the Unchangeable God; Well, and what then? Why, *My Glory will I not give to another, nor my Praise to Graven Images*; my Glory shall not die, but live; my Glory shall not be always veiled and eclipsed, but it shall shine forth in perfect Lustre and Splendor. One of the great Burthens that lyes upon the People of God, is the Sufferings of his Name and Glory, *The Reproaches of them that reproached thee are fallen upon me*, (says David) Psal. 69. 9. God's Glory is veiled, his Name is blasphemed, his Worship is interrupted, his Providence is denied, all his Attributes are obscured, and his Honour every way thrown in the Dust, which makes Holy Souls go mourning from Day to Day: But, my Beloved, here is that may comfort the Soul, God is unchangeable, and therefore his Glory shall live, and shine forth again, the Veil shall in due time be taken away, and his Glory shall appear; yea, it shall be as eminently Illustrated and Displayed, as ever it has been Veiled and Eclipsed. You know how God speaks in Reference to the Glory of his Name, in Answer to Christ's Prayer, *Joh.* 12. 28. *Father, Glorifie thy Name*, (says Christ) and what Answer does the Father give him? *I have glorified it, and I will glorifie it again*, q. d. I have hitherto taken Care of my Glory, and I will take Care of it still. O, my Beloved, God's Glory has hitherto been dear to him, and he has hitherto maintained it in the World, and he is unchangeable, and therefore his Glory is as dear to him as ever it was, he is as jealous for it as ever, he is also every way as able to vindicate and maintain it as ever he was, and assure your selves, were it not that he knows how to make it shine forth so much the more illustriously and conspicuously afterwards, he would not suffer it to be so veiled and eclipsed as sometimes he does, yea, let me say, he is always carrying on, as the In-

E 5   terest

tereſt of his Peoples Happineſs, ſo the Concerns
of his own Glory.

2. God being unchangeab'e, his Church ſhall be
preſerved and delivered, preſerved under, and in
due time delivered out of, all her Troubles and
Afflictions, and what a Sweet Thing is that? The
poor Church of God is oftentimes plunged into
very deep and ſore Diſtreſſes, ſuch as are ready to
ſink and overwhelm Her, ſhe is oftentimes *afflicted,
toſſed with Tempeſts, and not comforted,* Iſa 45. 11.
Such indeed is Her Condition at this Day, and as
Good Old *Ely ſate trembling for the Ark of God,* a
Type of the Church, 1 Sam 4. 13. ſo it may be
ſome may now ſit trembling for the Church of
God, fearing how 'twill go with Her, and indeed
he is n't one of *Sion*'s Children that is not concerned for *Sion*'s Afflictions But lo! my Beloved,
in the midſt of all ſuch Fears and Tremblings of
Heart here is ſtrong Conſolation, God is unchangeable, and being unchangeable, he will certainly
ſupport and deliver his Church, and that in the
beſt Way and fitteſt Seaſon God has never yet
fail'd his Church in Her Afflictions Yea, 'tis ad-
mirable to conſider how hitherto he has carried
it towards Her under all Her Diſtreſſes, how ſweetly he has ſupported Her, and how ſeaſonably he
has delivered Her. When they were in *Ægypt,*
in the Iron Furnace, when they were in the Wil-
derneſs, when they were in the Red Sea, when
they were in *Babylon* in *Haman*'s time, and in *He-
rod*'s, when the Neck of the whole Church of God
was upon the Block at once, as it were, and alſo
all down along through the Times of Antichriſtian
Tyranny and Perſecution to this very Day, O
how Admirably has God wrought for them, both
in ſupporting and delivering of them? And certainly, what he has done, that he can and will do
for them again, as the Caſe ſhall require God is
unchangeable, *His Hand is not ſhortned, that he*

cannot save, nor his Ear grown heavy, that he cannot hear, *Isa.* 59. 1. God being unchangeable, he is as tender of, and careful for, his Church and People as ever he was; being unchangeable, every way the same to his People now as he was formerly, the same in his Love to them, his Jealousie for them, his Sympathy with them, and his Interest in them, he stands in the same Covenant-Relation to them that ever he did; he is their King, their Head, their Husband, their Friend, their Father, their Shepherd, now as well as heretofore, and he is every way as able to help them, and accordingly will support, and in due time deliver, them, and this Faith sees and rests assured of, *Isa.* 51. 9, 10, 11, 12. *Awake, awake, put on Strength, O Arm of the Lord, awake, as in the antient Days, in the Generations of old; art thou not it that hath cut* Rahab, *and wounded the Dragon? Art thou not it which hath dried the Sea, the Waters of the great Deep, that hath made the Depths of the Sea a Way for the ransomed to pass over* &c. So again, 2 *Cor.* 1. 9, 10. *But we had the Sentence of Death in our selves, that we should not trust in our selves, but in God who raiseth the Dead, who delivereth us from so great a Death, and doth deliver, in whom we trust that he will yet deliver us.* Mark, Faith, you see, argues from what God has done, to what he will do, for his poor Church and People, and what Bottom or Ground has it so to do but his Unchangeableness? Let *Sion* therefore, the Church and People of God, take heed of that Language, which he spake of old, *Isa.* 49 14. Sion *said, the Lord hath forsaken me, and my God hath forgotten me* And as *Jacob* elsewhere, *My Way is hid from the Lord, and my Judgment is passed over by my God;* e'er God must change e'er this can be. True, God may permit his Church to be sorely afflicted, as at this Day, but 'tis but to Illustrate his own Glory the more in Her Support and Deliverance.

3. God

3. God being unchangeable, his Enemies shall be destroyed, they shall all die and perish; I mean his incorrigible, implacable, Enemies, who will not stoop to the Scepter of his Kingdom. God may, and sometimes does, permit his and his Peoples Enemies to *Practise and Prosper,* and that for a long time together, he lets them alone in their Sins and Oppositions against both himself and them, yea, he even *fills their Belly with his hid Treasure,* (as you have it) *Psal.* 17. 14. he lets them injoy some of the best of outward Comforts and Contentments, and that in great Fulness, which oftentimes proves a great Burthen and Temptation to his poor afflicted People, such as is ready even to sink and bear them down: So it was with the Psalmist, *Psal.* 73. beg. and 'tis so many times with us; but remember that God is unchangeable, and being unchangeable, though he may permit his and his Peoples Enemies to *Practise and Prosper* for a time, yet not always, no, they shall be destroyed, and that with a great Destruction: Pray observe how things issued at last in that very Psalm, *Psal.* 73. 10, &c. *Surely thou didst set them in slippery Places, thou castedst them down into Destruction, how are they brought into Desolation as in a Moment? They are utterly consumed with Terrors,* &c. Pray observe, he was not more offended at, nor was he more ready to envy their Prosperity before, than now he wonders at their Ruin and Destruction So *Psal.* 37. 35, &c. *I have seen the Wicked in great Power, and spreading himself like a green Bay-tree, yet he passed away, and lo! he was not: Yea, I sought him, but he could not be found, the Transgressors shall be destroyed together, the End of the Wicked shall be cut off.* So *Deut.* 32. 35, 35 *To me belongeth Vengeance and Recompence,* (says God in Reference to his and his Peoples Enemies) *their Foot shall slide in due time, for the Day of their Calamity is at hand, and the things which shall come upon them make haste,*

for

for the Lord shall judge his People, &c. Still you see, though God permit his and his Peoples Enemies to prosper for a time, yet at last they are destroyed, and as sure as God is unchangeable they shall be destroyed. Pray compare but my Text with the Verse immediately preceeding, *Mal* 3. 5, 6. *I will come near to you to Judgment,* (says God) *and I will be a swift Witness against the Sorcerers, and against the Adulterers, and against false Swearers, and against all that oppress the Hireling in his Wages, the Widow and the Fatherless, and that fear not me, saith the Lord;* q. d. I'll suddenly and terribly destroy all mine Enemies, all that go on in their Sinnings against me But how shall we be assured of this? He tells you in the next Words, for *I am the Lord, I change not,* q d. as sure as I am God and Unchangeable they shall be destroyed. O, Sirs, tho' God permits his and his Peoples Enemies to Prosper for a time, yet he always certainly destroys them in the Conclusion, and he will do so still, because he is unchangeable God is every way the same that ever he was, the same in Holiness, Jealousie, Justice, Power, that ever he was; He is as Holy now as ever he was, and so does hate Sin as much as ever he did: He is as just now as ever he was, and so as ready and propense to take Vengeance as ever; he is as jealous now, as jealous for his Name, Worship, Gospel, and People, as ever he was, and so will as little bear with the Opposers and Abusers of them, he is as wise and powerful now as ever, and so as able to deal with his Enemies: 'Tis a great Scripture that *Job* 9. 4. *He is wise in Heart, and mighty in Strength, who ever hard'ned himself against him and prospered?* O never any yet did, and never any shall. No, but *Psal.* 68. 21. *He will wound the Head of his Enemies, and the hairy Scalp of such an one as goeth on still in his Trespasses.* O that all the Enemies of God and his People, and all

Rebellious

Rebellious Impenitent ones would lay this to Heart.

4. God being unchangeable, the Purposes and Promises of his Grace to his Church and People shall certainly be accomplisht. God's Heart, my Beloved, has been full of Counsels and Purposes of Love towards his People from all Eternity, and he has also made many blessed Promises to them, *Promises* that are *exceeding Great and Precious*, 2 Pet. 1. 4. because full of exceeding Great and Precious Things Greatness and Preciousness do not often meet together, many things are Great, but then they are not Precious, and many things are Precious, but then they are not Great, but in the Promises of God to his Church and People Greatness and Preciousness do meet: Now look, whatever Purposes God has had in his Heart, and whatever Promises he has made in his Word to his People, they shall all be accomplisht, because he is an unchangeable God, he is the same now that he was when he took up those Purposes, and made those Promises, and therefore will assuredly make them all good in the due Season, and so much he tells us, (*Isa.* 46. 9, 10, 11. *I am God,* (says he) *and there is none else, I am God, and there is none like me, declaring the End from the Beginning, and from ancient times the things that are not yet done, saying, My Counsel shall stand, and I will do all my Pleasure; I have spoken, and I'll bring it to pass, I have purposed it, I will also do it:* Mark, first he asserts his Godhead and Unchangeableness, and then he tells you all his Pleasure shall stand and be accomplisht. God being unchangeable (First) none can turn him, or make him alter his Mind, Job 23. 13, 14 *He is in one Mind, and who can turn him? And what his Soul desireth, even that he doth; for he performeth the thing that is appointed for me, &c.* The wisest and most resolved among Men may possibly be wrought upon, and brought over from

that

what they purposed, but 'tis not so with God.
(Secondly) None can hinder him from or in his
making good his Purposes and Promises, *Isa.* 43.
13 *Before the Day was, I am he, and there is none
that can deliver out of my Hand : I will work, and
who shall let it ?* Poor Soul, whoever thou art,
that art one of the Lord's People, look back to the
Eternal Counsels and Purposes of his Love towards
thee, and thou wilt find them a great Deep, a
Fountain of Infinite Sweetness, in them thou wilt
see Heaps of Love, and Treasures of Grace ; and
then turn thine Eye to the Promises of his Covenant, which thou wilt find unexpressively sweet,
and exactly suitable to thy Condition, to all thy
Wants, and then know assuredly that the whole,
both of the one and the other, shall be accomplisht to thee in due Season. 'Tis true indeed,
his Counsels may seem to us to be frustrated, and
his Promises may for a time be deferred and de-
layed, insomuch that our hasty unbelieving Hearts
may be ready to conclude, that they will never be
accomplisht, saying with the *Psalmist, Does his
Promise fail for evermore ? Psal.* 77. 8. But, Soul,
wait a while, and they shall all be made good to
a Tittle. Has he promised to pardon thee, to
cleanse thee, to give thee a new Heart, and a new
Spirit, to write his Law in thine Heart ? Has he
promised to save thee, and lodge thee at last in
his own Bosom ? Then know it shall all be accomplisht. Oh how sweet is this! Oh to fasten upon
a Promise, and see it sure to be made good, as in
God's Unchangeableness we may, there we may
see all as sure as if 'twere already accomplisht. Oh
what strong Consolation does this afford ? What
unexpressible Sweetness will this give unto a Soul ?

5. God being unchangeable, the Saints are unchangeably Happy, and have a blessed *Asylum* to
flee unto under all those Changes and Emergencies

that may at any time come upon them. Pray
mark, my Beloved, God is the Saint's God and
Portion, and in him does their Happiness lye, he
therefore being unchangeable, they have an unchangeable Happiness, they are an Happy People, and
they will be unchangeably so. *The Counsel of the
Lord standeth for ever, the Thoughts of his Heart to
all Generations,* and what then? *Blessed is the Nation whose God is the Lord, and the People whom he
hath chosen for his own Inheritance,* Psal. 33. 11, 12.
The Saints (as one well observes) are in all Respects a Blessed People, they are Blessed in the
Pardon of their Sins *Blessed is the Man whose Sins
are forgiven,* Psal. 32. 1. They are Blessed in Regard of the Disposition of their Souls. *Blessed are
the Poor in Spirit, blessed are the Meek, blessed are
they that hunger and thirst after Righteousness,* Mat.
5. 3, 4. 6. They are Blessed in their Obedience,
and Walking with God. *Blessed are the Undefiled in
the Way,* Psal. 119. 1. They are Blessed in their
Hopes and Expectations *Blessed are they that
wait for God,* Isa. 30. 18. Thus they are every
Way, and in all Respects, a Blessed People, but
here lyes the Perfection and Top Glory of their
Blessedness, and what indeed comprehends all the
rest in it, namely, that the unchangeable God is
their God and Portion *Happy is the People whose
God is the Lord,* Psal. 144. 15. Oh, this speaks
them to be infinitely and unchangeably Happy, and
accordingly they should live upon him, and that
under all their Streights and Difficulties. Oh, Sirs,
what is there that this will not support and comfort you under? Do your Friends and Comforts
here change? However, God, your best Friend and
Comfort, changes not, and that is enough. Do times
and Seasons change, and that for the worse, from
Sunshine to Storms? Well, however, Soul, thy
God changes not, and that is enough to sweeten
all.

all. Doft thou thy felf change? *Changes and War are upon thee*, and which is the worft of it, thy Spirit changes, it will not keep even with God one Hour, well, ftill thy God changes not, and that is enough. Do new Temptations arife, and old Corruptions break out anew? Does Guilt revive, and recur upon thee? Be it fo, yet thy God is unchangeable, and fo can and will relieve and fuccour thee now as well as formerly, and that is enough. Yea, do God's Difpenfations change towards thee? He did fmile, now he frowns; he did lift up, now he cafts down; the Light of his Countenance did fhine brightly upon thee, now 'tis veil'd and clouded: Well, however, thy God himfelf changes not; his Heart, his Counfel, his Covenant, his Love, are ftill the fame towards thee that ever they were, howbeit the Difpenfation be changed. Oh, this One Word, God is Mine, and he is Unchangeable, has Infinite Sweetnefs in it, and it fpeaks me to be Infinitely and Unchangeably Happy. Oh you that are the People of God, labour to fee and rejoice in this Happinefs of yours: Which that you may the better do, let me add only Two fhort Words to this, and I will fhut up the whole Difcourfe.

1. Confider, that as your God is unchangeable, fo you are unchangeably interefted in him. This unchangeable God is unchangeably your God; what, though God be unchangeable, (may fome poor Soul fay) what will that avail me? My Intereft in him, I fear, will change and fail, there will fhortly be an end of that: No, Soul, the unchangeable God being indeed thine, he is thine for ever: So the Church, *This God is our God for ever and ever, Pf.* 48.14. O Soul, thou through Infinite, Free, and Rich, Grace, haft a Covenant-Intereft in, and Relation to, the unchangeable God, and this Intereft and Relation of thine is a firm, lafting,

lasting, and unchangeable, Interest and Relation.
Nothing that either Men, Devils, or Lusts, can do,
can possibly break or null it. And so he tells us,
Psal. 89. 30, 31, 32. of which we have spoken
before. I shall here only add a Saying or Two of
Austin, *The Chief Good,* (says he) *which is God, is
neither given to such as are unwilling to have him, nor
taken away from such as are unwilling to part with
him ·* And elsewhere, *No Man does or can lose thee,
O God,* (says he) *unless he that is unwilling to lose
thee, and go without thee, and he that willingly parts
with thee, whither does he go ? Whither does he flee ?
But from thee smiling, to thee frowning, from thee a
reconciled Father, to thee an angry Judge ?* O Soul,
as long as thou art willing to have God thine, so
long he shall be thine, yea, more, thine Interest
in him depends not upon thy Willingness of it,
but upon his unchangeable Love and Covenant,
and his Love and Covenant both must change, e'er
thine interest in him can fade and change.

2. Consider, as your God is unchangeable, so
after a while you shall unchangeably enjoy him,
and be with him, your Vision and Fruition of him
shall be unchangeable. *Our Happiness* (says *Austin*)
*is begun here in Election, but 'tis perfected hereafter in
Fruition.* You that have chosen the unchangeable
God, you shall after a few Days enjoy the God
whom you have chosen, your Happiness is great
in your chusing of him, but how much more great
will it be in your enjoying of him? *Psal.* 73. 24,
25. *Thou shalt guide me by thy Counsels, and afterwards receive me unto Glory, whom have I in Heaven but thee, and there is none upon Earth I desire be-
side thee, q. d.* I have chosen, and I do again chuse,
thee for my God and Portion, and some Enjoyment I have of thee here, and more I shall have
hereafter in Heaven, I shall e'er long be taken to
enjoy thee in thy Glory, fully, immediately, and

for ever, for thou art mine, and I have made a Solemn Choice of thee. O Saints, the unchangeable God is yours, and fome Communion you have with him here in the Ways of his Grace, which is Sweet and Happy, but after you have enjoyed him in the Ways of his Grace a while here, you fhall be taken to the unchangeable Enjoyment of him in his Glory above, which will be infinitely more Sweet and Happy, your Enjoyment of him here is low and remote, as well as changeable and unconftant, but your Enjoyment of him Above will be full, clofe, and unchangeable: Here you have now and then a gracious Vifit from him, he vifits you in this Duty, and that Ordinance, in this Mercy, and in that Affliction, but Oh how fhort many times are thofe Vifits of his? Alas! he is gone again in a Moment. But after a while you fhall enjoy him in his Glory, and there you fhall not have a fhort Vifit now and then only, but his conftant Prefence for ever. *We fhall be ever with the Lord*, 1 *Thef.* 4. 17. Oh Bleffed Souls! There he will unchangeably delight in you, unchangeably fhine upon you, unchangeably communicate himfelf in his Grace and Glory to you, Oh how Sweet and Bleffed will this be! Well, for a Clofe of all, Saints, the unchangeable God is unchangeably your God, and howbeit your Vifions of him be yet but dark, and your Communion with him but low, yet wait a while, and the Day will break, and all your Shadows fhall flee away, you fhall change your ebbing Waters for a full Tide, your Glimmerings and Dawnings fo a Noon-day, your imperfect Beginnings for a full and perfect Confummation of Communion with him. Howbeit there be now a Veil upon his Face, that you cannot behold him, yet wait a while, and the Veil fhall be taken away, and you fhall behold his Face, his Glory, for ever, and that fo as to be fully changed

into

into the Image thereof, and eternally folaced and
fatisfied therein, fuitable to that Word, *Pſal.* 17.
15. (with which I'll cloſe all) *As for me, I will be-*
hold thy Face in Righteouſneſs; I ſhall be ſatisfied when
I awake with thy Likeneſs. Amen.

THE
Crue Reſt:
OR,
The Souls Reſt in GOD,

Opened -and Improved from
PSAL. 116. 7.
Return unto thy Reſt, O my Soul.

CHAP. I.

An Introduction to the Words. What that Reſt is
which David *calls upon his Soul to return unto.*
The Sum of the Words, and of our Intendment from
them, laid down in one general Poſition.

IT is the great Happineſs of the Saints, that howbeit they meet with many fore Troubles and
Afflictions here in this World; yea, though they
meet with little elſe but Trouble and Affliction
here, yet there is a Reſt to come for them, a Sweet
Reſt, a Bleſſed Reſt, a Glorious Reſt, a Reſt not
liable to either Decay or Diſturbance for ever: So
the

the Apoftle tells us, *Heb.* 4. 9. *There remaineth a Reft to the People of God :* Nor is this all their Happineſs; for not only does there remain a Reft for them hereafter, but there is alfo a Reft, a Sweet Reft, a Bleffed Reft, which they do, or may, attain unto here, a Reft even in the midſt of all thofe Troubles, which here they are expofed unto: And Bleffed be God for this Reft ; Reft is fweet, but Reft in Trouble, Reft in the midſt of many and fore Troubles, Oh how Sweet, how Glorious, is this! Now this is the Reft which I would a little contemplate and fpeak unto, as the proper Subjeƈt of thefe Words of the *Pfalmiſt, Return unto thy Reſt, O my Soul:* Which Words are *David's* Call or Command to his Soul to return unto its Reft: And the only thing to be enquired into for the clearing of them, and therein for the making Way to what we intend from them, is, what this Reft is which *David* here calls upon his Soul to return unto; and I find it expounded Two Ways.

1. Some expound it of God himfelf, God in Chriſt, who indeed is the Reft, as well as the Refuge, of his People: God is *centrum quietativum,* (as the Schools fpeak) the proper, quieting, refting, Center of the Soul, and in him alone can it truly reft Thus *Vatablus,* a Learned Man, expounds it; *Return unto thy Reſt, O my Soul;* that is, (fays he) *Return to him with whom thou wilt find the moſt perfeƈt Reſt, to wit, unto God :* Indeed with him, and in him, alone is perfeƈt Reft to be found, as in its Place may be fhewn.

2. Others expound it of a quiet, ſerene, fedate, well compofed, Frame and Pofture of Soul ; and thus *Calvin* and others expound it : *That ſome Interpreters* (fays he) *do by Reſt here underſtand God, is ſtrained ; 'tis rather to be taken fo a tranquil and well-compoſed Frame of Soul :* And indeed the Scope of

of the Context looks this Way, for mark, David
had been in great Affliction, *The Sorrows of Death*
had compaſſed him about, and the Pains of Hell had
got hold upon him, as you find *Verſ.* 3. and hereup
on there had followed, as is too probable, great
Perplexity of Spirit within, great Murmurings and
Tumults, Frettings and Diſcompoſures, in his Soul;
and now he calls off his Soul from thoſe unquiet
Motions and Agitations, and commands it to re
turn to Reſt, that is, to a calm, quiet, ſerene,
ſedate, and well-compoſed Frame again. Thus al
ſo another Judicious Interpreter expounds it; *Re-*
turn unto thy Reſt, O my Soul; as if he ſhould ſay,
O my Soul, hitherto thou haſt been toſſed up and down,
among the Waves and Storms of Sorrows, Doubts, and
Deſperation; thou haſt been greatly afflicted and di-
ſturbed, when the Sorrows of Death and Hell did preſs
in upon thee, and ſometimes ſuch has been the Caſe
with thee, that thou couldeſt ſee no Port, no Haven,
in which thou mighteſt reſt; but now theſe Storms be-
ing over and gone, and a Port opening it ſelf to thy
Faith, in which thou mayeſt Reſt, now put in and return
to thy Reſt, now be quiet and joyful, as knowing where
thou oughteſt to reſt. Thus this Reſt is doubly ex
pounded. Now I ſhall exclude neither of theſe
Senſes, but rather joyn them both together, and
by Reſt here underſtand the Soul's being at Reſt in
God, in whom alone Reſt is to be found for Souls:
Nor am I alone in ſo doing, for I find a Learned
Man ſo to underſtand it, *Return unto thy Reſt, O my*
Soul, that is, (ſays he) be no longer filled with
Diſquietment and Perturbation, but acquieſce and
ſit down ſatisfied in God, thy Reſt and Portion for
ever Accordingly take the Sum of the whole, and
ſo of my Intendment in this Poſition.

Doct

Doct. *That the Souls of the Saints ſhould be at Reſt in God: Or, the Frame and Poſture of Soul the Saints ſhould live in, is a Frame and Poſture of Reſt in God.*

Whatever the Saints Condition may be, or whatever Diſpenſations they may be exerciſed withal, yet ſtill their Souls ſhould be at Reſt in God: *David's* Soul was for a time gone off its Reſt, 'twas gone off from that Sedateneſs, Compoſure, and Satisfaction, which it was wont to have in God; his Condition was full of Trouble and Diſturbance, and his Soul was filled with Trouble and Diſturbance too, but here tacitly at leaſt he rebukes his Soul for this, and expreſly commands it to return to Reſt again, to a Reſt in God, and that as its proper Poſture; for mark how he ſpeaks, *Return unto* [*thy Reſt*] *O my Soul,* [thy Reſt] the proper Poſture of the Souls of the Saints is to be at Reſt in God, and that Poſture they ſhould be in at all times, and in all Conditions. What the Soul's Reſt in God is, what Obligations the Saints are under to be thus at Reſt in God, the Sweetneſs and Excellency of the Frame, with a Call to all to live in this Frame and Poſture, and Helps in Order thereunto, are the Things which will properly fall under Conſideration in our Procedure on this Argument.

CHAP. II.

What the Soul's Reſt in God is, opened, and when the Soul may be ſaid to be at Reſt in Him.

BUT what is it for a Soul to be at Reſt in God, or to live in a Poſture of Reſt in God? In general 'tis for a Soul to ſit down ſatisfied with

what

what God does as best, and with what God is, as all; and so this Rest of the Soul in God lyes in Two things. (First) In a free and chearful Submission to the Divine Will and Providence. (Secondly) In a full and ample Satisfaction in and with the Divine Presence and Fulness. And Oh the Beauty, the Sweetness, the Amiableness, that both these carry in them! A little of each.

1. 'Tis to sit down satisfied with what God doth as best, and so it lyes in a free and chearful Submission to the Divine Will and Providence, the Will and Providence of God concerning him : The Soul, through Grace, gets right Apprehensions of God's Will and Providence concerning him, he looks upon the Will of God to be Sovereign, a Righteous, a Wise, and a Good, Will, and hereupon he sits down satisfied with it, whatever it does with him, whatever it allots and orders out concerning him.

1. The Soul looks upon the Will and Providence of God concerning him to be a Sovereign Will and Providence, a Will and Providence, which does, which may do, with him whatever it pleases, and so he acquiesces in it. *It is the Lord,* (said Good old *Ely*) *let him do what seemeth him good,* 1 *Sam.* 3. 18. Mark how he bows and submits his Soul to the Divine Will and Providence, it is the Lord, it is a Sovereign God, a God that may do with me and mine whatever he will; and in the Sense of this his Soul freely submits. It was a dreadful and terrible Message which *Samuel* told him from the Lord, but so dreadful and terrible as it was, yet having his Eye upon the Sovereignty of God, he freely acquiesces. Suitable whereunto is the Observation of a Learned Man upon this Place, *Eli* (saith he) *in these Words expresses great Patience, and a great Consent or Agreement with the Divine Will, he did not expostulate with God, but humbly*

humbly *complied and comported with him.* God, my Beloved, has an absolute Sovereignty over us all, and may do with us as he pleases . 'Tis what he challenges to himself, as his Prerogative , *All Souls are mine,* (says he) *Ezek* 18. 4. mine, to do with them, to difpose of them, as I will: And you know how God afferts this his Sovereignty in *Jer.* 18. 6. *O Houfe of Ifrael, cannot I do with you as the Potter ?* (fays the Lord) *Behold, as the Clay is in the Potter's Hand, fo are ye in my Hand, O Houfe of* Ifrael. Pray mark, he had before, at *Verf.* 4. fhewn them how the Potter dealt by the Clay, and what an abfolute Power he had over it, making it a Veffel, and marring it again, as he pleafed ; and now here in *Verf.* 6. fays he, *Cannot I do with you as this Potter* doth with his Clay ? I can, *behold, as the Clay is in the Hand of the Potter, fo are ye in mine Hand ,* i. e I have an abfolute Power over you, to do with you, and difpofe of you, as I fee good, and I may make or marr you upon the Wheel of my Providence as I pleafe · And you know how God by the Apoftle argues in that greateft of Cafes, *Rom.* 9. 21. *Hath not the Potter Power over the Clay, of the fame Lump to make one Veffel unto Honour, and another unto Difhonour ?* In which Words God afferts his abfolute Sovereignty to difpofe of all Men as to their Eternal Eftates as he pleafes : Thus he has an abfolute Sovereignty over all : Now the Holy Soul apprehending this Sovereignty in God, falls under the Awe and Dread of it, and accordingly acquiefces in his Will, whatever it be.

2. The Soul looks upon the Will and Providence of God concerning him to be an Holy and Righteous, as well as a Sovereign, Will and Providence, and upon that Account alfo acquiefces therein. *The Lord is Righteous,* (faid the Church) *Lam.* 1. 18. *The Lord is Righteous, for I have rebelled*

F   *againft*

againſt his Commandment ; *q. d.* 'Tis true, my Sorrow is great, and mine Affliction heavy , but God
is Juſt and Holy in it, 'tis no more than, nor in
Truth ſo much as, my Sins have deſerved . Indeed, God's Dealings with her were very terrible
and amazing , but yet, apprehending the Righteouſneſs of God in them, She ſubmits to him under
all: So *Dan.* 9. 7. *O Lord, Righteouſneſs belongeth
unto thee, but unto us Confuſion of Face :* They ſaw
the Righteouſneſs of God in his Dealings with
them, and ſo were at Reſt in his Will. *God is
Righteous* (the Scripture tells us) *in all his Ways,
and Holy in all his Works,* and *he is a Juſt Lord that
doth,* that can do, no Wrong, *no Iniquity,* Zeph 3.
5. Now the Holy Soul gets a Sight of this, and
is awed with the Senſe thereof, and accordingly
acquieſces in God's Will· True, (ſays he) this and
that is ſharp, it ſmarts ſorely, it runs croſs to my
carnal Appetite, to my Senſe and Reaſon ; but I
am ſure God is Holy and Juſt in all, I have deſerved all and more at his Hand , and in the
Senſe of this he acquieſces in his Will, and is ſatisfied with his Dealings.

3. The Soul looks upon the Will and Providence
of God concerning him to be a Wiſe, as well as
an Holy, Will and Providence, and thereupon alſo
bows to it, and acquieſces in it. God, my Beloved, is *the only Wiſe* God, and all his Works are
done in Wiſdom; his Will is a Wiſe Will, a Will
guided and ordered by Counſel, he *works all
things according to the Counſel of his own Will,* Eph.
1. 11. God is never out in what he does, but does
all as becomes an Only and an Infinitely Wiſe
God , which the Holy Soul getting a Sight and
Senſe of, he freely acquieſces in whatever the
Will of God is concerning him, and reſts fully ſatisfied with what God does : In *Job* 1. 22 we read
*that in all this Job ſinned not, neither charged he God
fooliſhly*

foolishly : *In all this,* that is, in all his Trials and Afflictions, though many, though great, (*in all this Job sinned not, neither charged he God foolishly;* or, (as you have it in the Margent of some of your Bibles) *he did not attribute Folly to God,* he sinned not by attributing of Folly to God, but he worshipped and adored the Divine Wisdom, the Wisdom of God, in all his Dealings with him, he acquitted God's Providence of Folly, and bowed to the Infinite Wisdom thereof, and was satisfied with all as best for him : All this, says the Holy Soul, is the Work of a Wise Will, regulated by Counsel, true, all runs cross to my Will and my outward Interest, but 'tis all ballanced by Infinite Wisdom, and I am satisfied therewith : Thus he is at Rest in God.

4. The Soul looks upon the Will and Providence of God concerning him to be a Good, as well as a Wise, Will and Providence, and thus also acquiesces in it. The *Psalmist* tells us, that *all the Paths of the Lord are Mercy and Truth, to such as keep his Covenant and his Testimonies,* Psal. 25. 10. By the *Paths* of the Lord here we are to understand his Providences: Now (says he) these are all Mercy and Truth to his People ; not some, but *all,* of them, even the hardest and severest, the most dark, terrible, and killing of them, they are *all Mercy and Truth,* Mercy it self, and Truth it self · Whatever the Will and Providence of God brings forth, yet to his People there is Love in all, Goodness in all, Faithfulness in all, and the Holy Soul getting a Sight thereof, sweetly acquiesces, and is at Rest in whatever God does: So *David,* Psal. 119. 75. *I know, O Lord, that thy Judgments are right, and that thou in Faithfulness hast afflicted me.* See *Hezekiah* also, *Isa.* 39. 8. *Good* (says he to *Isaiah*) *is the Word of the Lord which thou hast spoken.* 'Twas a sharp and a severe Word or Message

fage which God by *Isaiah* sent him, as you may
see in the precedent Verses, but yet he saw Goodness in all, and Kindness in all, and accordingly
acquiesced therein. Truly there is Love and Goodness in all God's Dealings with his People, and the
Holy Soul seeing it, his Language is, whether God
fills or empties, whether he gives or takes away,
whether he lifts up or casts down, whether he
kills or makes alive ; yet there is Love in all,
Goodness in all, and 'tis best for me : God chuses
for me, and disposes of me, better than I could
for my self, and I am satisfied with what he does
Thus the Soul gets right Apprehensions of the Will
and Providence of God concerning him, and
hereupon is sweetly Satisfied, and sits down at Rest
in God, in the midst of all he does to him or with
him. True, God may deal somewhat severely
with him, he may *break him with Breach upon
Breach*, as he did *Job* He may *cause all his Waves
and his Billows to pass over him*, as he dealt with
David , but still the Soul looks upon all to be Holy, Just, and Good, and no other than what God
in his Sovereignty may do, and so he rests satisfied therewith, he rests content in God and his
Will under all, there are no Disquietments or Per-
plexities of Spirit, no Distractions or Discompo-
sures of Soul, no Frettings, no Tumults, no Murmurings, no Risings of Heart against God or his
Will, but there is a sweet Calm, Serenity, and
Rest, in the Soul , he is in a sedate, serene, Posture in his God, and this Rest in God the Psalmist speaks of, *Psal.* 37. 7. *Rest in the Lord, and
wait patiently for him* ; *fret not thy self because
him that prospereth in the Way* : Resting in God
here opposed to Fretting, and so must note a
quiet, sedate, well-composed, Spirit in God.

2. 'Tis for a Soul to sit down satisfied with what
God is, as all, and so it lyes in a full and ample Satisfaction

risfaction in and with the Divine Prefence and
Fulnefs: 'Tis for a Soul to take up in and with the
Bleffed God, as his Only and All-fufficient Portion
and Happinefs for ever. God, my Beloved, is an
All-fufficient God, he afferts his own All fufficien-
cy, *Gen.* 17. 1. *I am God All-fufficient,* (fays he to
Abraham) q. d. I am infinitely fufficient for my
felf, and I am infinitely fufficient for thee and all
my People, to make the one and the other Happy
for ever. God is an Inexhauftible Fountain of
Light, Life, Love, Bleffednefs, Perfection, and
Glory; and there is all Good in God, and he that
has God has all. *To him that overcometh will I give
to inherit all things.* And how fo ? *I will be his God,*
Rev. 21. 17. He has all Good, all-Happinefs, in
him, and in him we may find all as in its Fountain-
fulnefs and Purity. Now the Soul feeing God to
be fuch a God, and withal looking upon him as
his God in Covenant, fits down fatisfied with him
alone, faying, I have enough, I have all, and fo
is at Reft in him, whether he has much or little,
anything or nothing of this World's Good , whether the Streams run high or low with him, yet
here is a Fountain of Infinite Sweetnefs and Bleffednefs, and he drinks there, and fatisfies himfelf
there, he fees the Fountain is fo full, that he
needs not the Streams to make him Happy, and
accordingly fits down fatisfied therewith, and is at
Reft Thus *David's* Soul was at Reft in God, *Pfal.*
16. 5, 6. *The Lord is the Portion of mine Inheritance,*
and of my Cup: Well, and what then ? Why, he
fits down at Reft in him, *the Lines* (fays he) *are*
fallen to me in pleafant Places, yea, I have a goodly
Heritage, I have enough, enough for Delight, and
enough for Satisfaction, I have as much as my
Soul can wifh or defire, fo *Pfal.* 17. 15. *As for*
me, I will behold thy Face in Righteoufnefs, I fhall be
fatisfied, when I awake, with thy Likenefs; in the

Verfe immediately preceding he had fpoken of
fome whofe Portion and Happinefs is in this
World, well, and pray, *David,* where, and in
what, is your Portion ? Your Happinefs? My Portion is in God, and my Happinefs is in God, (fays
he) in the Sight of God, and in the Likenefs of
God; let others take up their Reft, Portion, and
Happinefs, where, and in what, they will, God is
my Reft, my Portion, my Happinefs, my All, for
ever: *As for me, I will behold,* &c. Again, *The
Lord lives,* (fays he) *and bleffed be my Rock,* Pfal.
18. 46. *q. d.* fuch and fuch Comforts are dead and
gone, *they are not,* (as *Jacob* fpake of his Sons)
well, but however God lives ftill, I have a Living
God, and he is a Living Happinefs, and that's
enough. So 2 *Sam.* 23. 5. *Although my Houfe be
not fo with God, yet he hath made with me an everlafting Covenant, ordered in all things, and fure, and
this is all my Salvation, and all my Defire, q. d.* God
is my God by Covenant, and here is my Happinefs, even all that my Soul can wifh, and accordingly he is at Reft in his God And *Pf.* 73. 25, 26.
*Whom have I in Heaven but thee ? And there is none upon
Earth that I defire in Comparifon of thee : My Heart
and my Flefh faileth, but God is the Rock of my Heart,
and my Portion for ever.* How dark foever things
to be with him, yet he looking to his God, was
fatisfied and at Reft in him, and with him, as infinitely enough for him. The Prophet *Habakkuk*
refolved upon the fame Courfe, *Hab.* 3. 17, 18.
*Although the Fig-tree fhall not Bloffom, neither fhall
Fruit be in the Vines, the Labour of the Olive fhall
fail,* &c. *yet will I rejoice in the Lord, I will joy in
the God of my Salvation :* He fuppofes the worft
that could come, and yet ftill refolves to be at
Reft in God, and that God alone fhall be enough
for him, when all other things fail. Thus the
Holy Soul fits down fatisfied with God alone, fet-
ting

ting God, and an Interest in God, over and against
all his Wants, Losses, Burthens, Difficulties, Temptations, as one infinitely able to relieve and satisfie
him under all, his Language to God is, Lord, let
others take the World, and the good things thereof, give me thy self, and I have enough; run out
to broken Cisterns, who will let me have a free
Recourse unto the Fountain, and I am satisfied;
tis true, the Tide of Creature-comforts runs low
with me, and on the other Hand the Waves and
Surges of Affliction rise high, but God is All-sufficient, and I have enough in him, he sees a little of that Glorious Fulness, Sweetness, and Blessedness, that is in God, and hereupon sings an Holy Requiem unto himself, saying, Soul, take thine
Ease, thou hast Goods, Light, Life, Love, Blessedness, Salvation, enough laid up for thee for
many Days, yea, for the Days of Eternity, take
thine Ease, sit down satisfied in and with thy God
alone, hadst thou Ten Thousand Worlds, without him thou had'st nothing, but in him thou hast
all, rest thou therefore in him. Thus you see
what 'tis for a Soul to be at Rest in God, and when
he may be said to be at Rest in him.

CHAP. III.

The great Obligations the Saints are under, thus to
live at Rest in God. Several of these Obligations
insisted on, as the first Evidence of the Truth of our
Proposition.

HAving seen what 'tis for a Soul to be at Rest
in God, our next Work shall be to shew you
what Obligations the Saints are under, thus to live
at Rest in him, and that as an undeniable Evidence
of the Truth of our Position: The Saints are under mighty Obligations thus to be at Rest in God;
I shall insist only on Four, which are full of Weight,

and

and I beg they may accordingly affect and influence us.

1. The first Obligation the Saints are under to live at Rest in God, is this, The Blessed God hath freely made over himself in his Covenant to them, and that in all his Glorious Riches and Fulness, that in him their Souls might be at Rest. He hath given himself to them as their Rest and Portion, and is not this a mighty Obligation in the Case? God, my Beloved, in the Covenant of his Love, hath freely given and made over himself to his People in all his Riches and Fulness, in all his Excellencies and Perfections, to be used, possest, and enjoyed, by them, as an All-sufficient Rest, Portion, and Happiness, for ever: This is evident in the very Tenour of the Covenant, and where ever you have a formal Mention or Record of the Covenant in Scripture, this is put in, *I will be your God* · You have Three Great and Solemn Mentions of the Covenant in Scripture, and in all of them this is in. One is *Gen.* 17. 7. another is *Jer.* 31. 33, 34. and the third is *Heb.* 8. 10, 11, 12. In these Places you have the most express Records of the Covenant, God's Covenant with his People, that are in all the Scripture, and in all there is this, *I will be your God.* In the Two latter Places we have other Promises, Promises of Pardon, Cleansing, Teaching, and the like, but in that to *Abraham*, in *Genesis*, we have only this, *I'll be thy God*, for indeed this comprehends all the rest, and all the other Promises that are contained in the Covenant of God, are but Branches growing out of this Root, and do but open this to us   This (as one speaks) is *Caput Fœderis*, the Head or Top of the Covenant , *Anima Fœdris*, (as another) the Soul of the Covenant , *Substantia Fœderis*, (as another) the Life and Substance of the Covenant: and indeed when God says to a Soul, I'll be thy

God,

God, he does therein say, I'll pardon thee, I'll
cleanse thee, I'll teach thee, I'll save thee, I'll
make thee happy, for ever For God to be our
God, is for God to be and communicate all Good
to us, that a God can communicate, and Creatures
receive, 'tis for God to love us, to bless us, to
care for us, to make us happy, for ever ; 'tis for
God to give us eternal Life, to be a Friend, a Father, an Husband, and a Saviour, to us. '*Tis (as
Luther somewhere expounds it) for God to make
over himself in all his Excellencies, Perfections, and
Glory, his Wisdom, Power, Goodness, Faithfulness,
All-sufficiency, Unchangeableness, and Eternity, to his
People, as then Rest and Happiness, to be possest and
enjoyed by them for their Good for ever.* In a Word,
for God to say to a poor Creature, I will be thy
God, is as much as if he shou'd say, Look, whatever I am, that I will be to thee, and look,
whatever I can do, that I will do for thee, so far
as thou art capable of the one or the other, to
make thee Happy for ever · I am a Fountain of
Life, and such will I be to thee, I am a God of
Peace and Pardon, and such will I be to thee, I
am a God of Grace, of Love, yea, I am a God that
is Love it self, and such will I be to thee, I am
the Father of Mercies, and the God of all Grace,
and such will I be to thee, I'll beget new Mercies
for thee every Day I am a God of Comfort, yea,
of all Comfort, and such will I be to thee, I am
an Unchangeable, Eternal, All-sufficient, God, and
such will I be to thee. I can pardon guilty Souls,
break the hardest Hearts, enlighten the darkest
Minds, cleanse the impurest Spirits, I can make
unbelieving Hearts believing, I can support droop-
ing Spirits, and all this I'll do for thee : I can carry thee through Life and Death, and bring thee
safe to Heaven, and there communicate my self
to thee for ever, to the filling of thy Soul with Delight,

light and Satisfaction, and this will I do for thee;
and surely happy is the Soul that has thus the Lord
for his God, and well may he fit down satisfied
with him, and at rest in him. Now, my Beloved,
hath God made over himself in his Covenant to
his People, as their Rest, that in him they might
find Rest, and should they not be at Rest in him?
O Sirs, is not God enough for us? Has he laid himself under Bonds to us, to be a God to us, and to
do like a God for us? And should we not rest in
him, and satisfie our selves with him alone? Surely we should.

2. The Second Obligation the Saints are under
to live at Rest in God, is this, they have solemnly voucht and chosen, and often do vouch and
chuse, God to be their Rest and Happiness. As
God has freely made over himself in his Covenant
to them, so they have solemnly voucht and chosen
him, and often do solemnly vouch and chuse him,
to be their Rest and Happiness. When the Saints
first enter into Covenant with God, then do they
solemnly chuse and vouch him to be their God
and Portion, their Rest and Happiness. Their Language to God then is, Lord, thou shall be my
Lord, my Rest, my Portion, my Happiness, my
All, for ever, I will have none in Heaven, or on
Earth, but thy self. Thus *David* had chosen God,
and he puts his Soul in Mind of it, *Pfal.* 16. 2. O
my Soul, (says he) *thou hast said unto God, thou art
my Lord*, thou haft chosen God for thy God, thy
Portion, thy Happiness, and upon this Account
he calls his Soul to rest in God, and in him he rests,
v. 5 And as at their first entring into Covenant with God, so also often afterwards, upon several Occasions, do they chuse and vouch God for
their Rest, Portion, and Happiness, for ever, they
make new Choices of God, and do lay new Claims
to him as theirs, in their Procedure of their Walking

ing with him.—— Sometimes upon Occasion of outward Troubles and Afflictions, Difficulties and Distresses, they make a new Choice of God, and vouch him afresh for their Rest and Happiness: So *David*, Psal. 31. 14. *I trusted in thee, O Lord; I said, thou art my God:* Here he makes a new Choice of God, and lays a new Claim to him as his, and when, or upon what Occasion, was this? When he was surrounded with outward Troubles, as appears, *Verf.* 10, 11, 12, 13. *My Life is spent with Grief, and my Years with Sighing, I was a Reproach among all my Enemies, I am forgotten, as a dead Man out of Mind · I have heard the Slander of many, Fear was on every Side, they devised to take away my Life*, and being thus distrest, he flees to God, and chuses him afresh, and lays a fresh Claim to him: So again, *Psal.* 142. 4, 5. *I looked on my right Hand, and beheld, but there was no Man that would know me, Refuge failed me, no Man cared for my Soul:* Well, and what then ? Why he runs to God, and vouches him afresh for his. *I cried unto thee, O Lord, I said, thou art my Refuge and my Portion in the Land of the Living.* So the Church in her great Troubles and Afflictions does in like Manner *The Lord is my Portion,* (faith she) *Lam.* 3. 24.—— Sometimes upon Occasion of some Eminent Mercy or Deliverance wrought by God for them, they do make a new Choice of God, and vouch him afresh to be theirs. So those, *Exod.* 15. 2. *The Lord is my Strength and Song, and he is become my Salvation: He is my God, and I will prepare him an Habitation, my Father's God, and I will exalt him.* He wrought a signal Deliverance for them; he had carried them through the Red Sea, delivered them from *Pharaoh* and the *Egyptians,* whom he drowned for their Sakes, and now they sing a Song of Praise to God, and vouch him to be their God; they renew Covenant with God, and to their Choice of him, as their Rest, their Portion, their All, for ever. Thus the Church does, *Pfal.* 48. 14. *This God is our God for ever and ever, he will be our God and Guide even unto Death :* God had done great things for her, and hereupon she vouches him afresh for hers. *David* often does the like,—— sometimes again upon Occasion of some fresh Discoveries made of God in his Love and Beauty to them, or their being taken into some near and intimate Communion with him, then they chuse him afresh, and vouch him to be theirs afresh : So, *Pfal.* 73. 25, 26. the *Pfalmist,* whoever he was, did, *Whom have I in Heaven but thee ?* (says he to God) *and there is none upon Earth that I desire besides thee , thou art the Rock of my Heart, and my Portion for ever ·* Here is a new Choice of God made by this Holy Man , and upon what Occasion was it ? Why, he had been with God in his Sanctuary , that is, he had been conversing with God in his Word and Ordinances, he had had some new Displays and Discoveries of his Love, Beauty, and Excellency, made to him , and hereupon he chuses God afresh, and vouches him to be his All, both in Heaven and upon Earth. So, you know, when the Spouse had been led into the Banqueting House by Christ, and had had the Banner of his Love displayed over Her , when she had been feasted by him in his House of Wine, then she made a new Choice of Christ, and vouches him for hers afresh : *My Beloved is mine, and I am his, Cant.* 2. 6. Thus the Saints, both at first, and also often afterwards in their walking with God, have chosen, and do chuse, him to be their God and Portion, their Rest and Happiness, and should they not then rest in him ? Surely, this Choice of theirs calls aloud, and should be a mighty Obligation upon them, to live at Rest in God for ever.

3. The third Obligation the Saints are under to
                                                    live

live at Reſt in God, is this, God is at Reſt in
them: As the Saints have choſen God for their
Reſt, ſo God hath choſen them for his Reſt, and
his Soul is at Reſt in them: *Pſal.* 132. 13, 14. *The
Lord hath choſen Zion, he hath deſired it for his Habitation, this is my Reſt for ever, here will I dwell,
for I have deſired it.* Zion here is a Type of the
Church and People of God, and as ſuch God's
Soul is at Reſt in her, *This is my Reſt :* The Saints
are, and to Eternity will be, a Delight and Solace to the Soul of God, God is indeed delighted,
and at Reſt in his People, above all the Works of
his Hands, hence the Church is called *The Delight
of God, Iſa.* 62. 4. Hence alſo he is ſaid to *rejoice
over them with Joy, to reſt in his Love upon them, and
to joy over them with ſinging, Zeph.* 3. 18. God is
in ſome ſort more delighted and at Reſt in his
People, than in the Angels themſelves, and indeed he ſees a greater Beauty and Glory upon
them than upon the Angels; he looks upon the
Angels as ſtanding in their own Beauty, their
own Holineſs and Righteouſneſs only; but he
looks upon his Saints as ſtanding in, and cloathed
with, the Beauty and Righteouſneſs of Chriſt,
and that is much more Glorious than the Angels :
The Beauty and Righteouſneſs of the Angels is
the Beauty and Righteouſneſs but of Creatures ;
but the Beauty and Righteouſneſs of the Saints is
the Beauty and Righteouſneſs of him that is God-
man, God as well as Man, *Rom.* 1. 17. and on
this Account God's Soul is more at Reſt in them,
God is chiefly delighted and at Reſt in himſelf,
and the Perfections of his own Being, next to
himſelf his Soul is delighted and at Reſt in Chriſt,
as Mediator· *Behold mine Elect, in whom my Soul
delighteth,* (ſaith the Father of him) *Iſa.* 42. 1.
and next to Chriſt the Mediator, his Soul is at Reſt
in his Saints and People in and through Chriſt, he
looks

looks upon them not as they are in themſelves, but as they are in Chriſt, not as apart from Chriſt, but as made one with Chriſt, and ſo as ſhining in his Beauty, and cloathed with his Righteouſneſs, as participating in all his Amiableneſs, he looks upon them, not ſo much according to what they are at preſent, as according to what they are in the Counſels of his own Love, and what he intends to make them, and ſo they are *all Glorious,*both *within* and *without* , and accordingly he is delighted in them.   Now, is God's Soul at Reſt in them? And ſhould not their Souls be at Reſt in him? O what a mighty Obligation is this upon them always to be at Reſt in God!

4 The Fourth Obligation the Saints are under to live at Reſt in God, is this; They hope to, and aſſuredly ſhall live at. Reſt in God, and with God for ever in Heaven· Heaven is a State of Reſt ; ſo the Apoſtle repreſents it; *There remaineth a Reſt to the People of God, Heb. 4. 9.* 'tis a State of Reſt in God, and with God, and in this Reſt the Saints hope to live, and live for ever. Hence they are ſaid to *have this Hope   Every one that hath this Hope,* 1 Joh. 3 3. *this Hope,* that is, the Hope of ſeeing Chriſt, and being made like him in the other World, the Hope of Heaven, the Eternal Reſt· Saints then are Perſons that have this Hope, hence alſo Heaven, and the Reſt to come, is called *Hope, the Hope which is laid up for you,* Col. 1. 5. and *the Bleſſed Hope, looking for the Bleſſed Hope, Tit.* 2. 13. In both theſe Places Heaven and the coming Reſt is called *Hope,* for *Hope* here (as *Calvin* and others obſerve) is put for the Object of Hope, or the God hoped for· But why is it called Hope? For this among other Reaſons, becauſe 'tis the great Object of the Saints Hopes, 'tis what they hope, and look, and long, for· And as they hope to, ſo aſſuredly they ſhall live at, Reſt in God, and

and with God for ever, 'tis what remains to them, and they ſhall in due time attain unto it : Hence 'tis ſaid to be *laid up for them in Heaven,* in that prequoted Place, *Col. 1. 5.* which (as *Calvin* alſo obſerves) notes the Certainty of it, and of their Enjoying of it, 'tis what they cannot miſs of, when the Apoſtle ſpeaks of an *Hope laid up in Heaven for us*; *he ſignifies to us, that the Saints ought therefore to reſt ſure and certain of the Promiſe of eternal Life, as if they had a Treaſure already hid, and laid up in a moſt ſafe Place.* Now do the Saints hope to, and accordingly ſhall they live at, Reſt in God and with God for ever, and ſhould they not be at Reſt in God here? Surely this is a mighty Obligation upon them to be always at Reſt in him. Thus you have ſeen ſome of thoſe Obligations the Saints lye under to live at Reſt in God, which though but ſome of them, yet are ſufficient to evince the Truth of our Poſition, namely, that they ſhould always be at Reſt in him.

CHAP. IV.

The Truth aſſerted; further evidenced from the Excellency of this Frame of Soul, the Worth and Excellency whereof is diſcovered in ſeveral Particulars.

AS the Saints are under many great and weighty Obligations to be always at Reſt in God, ſo to be always at Reſt in God is a Choice and an Excellent Frame and Poſture of Soul for the Saints to live in, 'tis indeed the beſt and moſt becoming Frame of Soul, they can poſſibly be found in in this world, which may give further Evidence to our Aſſertion. Now I ſhall ſhew you a little of the Worth and Excellency of this Frame and Poſture of Soul in a few Scripture Propoſitions about it.

1. To be at Reſt in God is a very Gracious Frame and Poſture of Soul, a Frame and Poſture of Soul which carries much of the Life and Power of

of Grace and Godliness in it . And O what an Excellent Frame and Posture must this then be? The more of the Life and Power of Grace and Godliness any Frame or Posture of Soul carries in it, the more Excellent it is ; now there is no Frame nor Posture of Soul, that I know of, which carries more of the Life and Power of Grace and Godliness in it than this of being at Rest in God does : Herein indeed does the main, if not the whole, of the Life and Power of Grace and Godliness consist ; for pray, what is Grace and Godliness, and wherein doth it consist, but in an holy Subjection to, and Acquiescence in, the Blessed God ? To bow and submit to God, as our Lord, and to chuse and acquiesce in God, as our Happiness, this is Grace, this is Godliness ; both which I take to be comprehended in *Psal.* 6 2. where *David* puts his Soul in Mind that he had both given up himself to God, and also chosen him for his Happiness, saying, *O my Soul, thou hast said unto the Lord, thou art my Lord,* my Ruler, my Happiness. This, my Beloved, is Grace or Godliness ; and the more of this there is found in us, the more Gracious we are, and what is this, but to be at Rest in God as we have opened it ? A restless and unquiet Spirit argues much of the Power of Sin, and shews that Grace has gotten but little, if any, Dominion in the Soul , and therefore 'tis made both the Character and Judgment of wicked Men, that they cannot rest: *The Wicked* (saith the Prophet) *are like the troubled Sea when it cannot rest, whose Waters cast up Mire and Dirt, there is no Peace to the Wicked, Isa.* 57. 20, 21. 'Tis meant of their own inward Unquietness and Restlesness of Spirit *Calvin* hereby understands *perpetuas animæ exagitationes atque perturbationes,* perpetual Tossings and Perturbations of Mind , and he speaks (I remember) thus. *This Simile of a Sea is an Elegant Similitude, and most apt to set forth the Inquietude of wicked Men,*

Men; for the Sea is troubled in it self, though it be not driven by Winds, nor toffed with Storms and Tempeft, but its own Waves fight one with another, and break one another; in like manner wicked Men are troubled with inteftine Evil, which is fixt and rooted in their own Minds. Thus a reftlefs, unquiet, Spirit argues much of the Power of Sin in the Soul, and fhews that Grace has got but little, if any, Dominion there · So on the other Hand, a Spirit at Reft in God muft carry much of the Life and Power of Grace and Godlinefs in it. This indeed is a great Part of the Kingdom of God; for *the Kingdom of God* (the Apoftle tells us) *confifts not in Meats and Drinks, but in Righteoufnefs, in Peace, and in the Joys of the Holy Ghoft,* Rom. 14. 17. *In Peace,* that is, (as a Learned Man expounds it) in an Holy Reft, and Quiet of Soul in God.

2. To be at Reft in God, is a ready Frame and Pofture of Soul, a Frame and Pofture of Soul, which renders a Man ready and prepared for every Call of God to him; and muft not that be an Excellent Frame? God, my Beloved, may call us to what he pleafes, to what Services he pleafes, and to what Conditions he pleafes; he may call us to what Services he pleafes; befides the general Duties of Chriftianity which are incumbent upon all, he may call us to what fpecial Work and Services he pleafes; he may call us to do, and he may call us to fuffer, and 'tis a Bleffed Thing to be fitted and prepared for the Call of God, and who more fo than he that lives at Reft in him? Alas, to fuch an one no Work, no Duty, no Service, is unfeafonable, fuch an one is fit to Pray, and fit to Praife, fit to Hear, and fit to Meditate; fit to fearch his own Heart, and fit to enquire into the Counfels of God, he is fit to do, and fit to fuffer the Will of God *My Heart is fixed, O God, my Heart is fixed;* or, (as you have it in the
Margin

Margin of some of your Bibles) *my Heart is pre-pared, O God, my Heart is prepared, Pful.* 57. 7. If you look back upon the firſt Verſe, you will find his Soul ſweetly at Reſt in God, *For* (ſays he) *O God, my Soul truſteth in thee, in the Shadow of thy Wings will I make my Refuge*, and being thus at Reſt in God, his Heart is prepared. 'Tis in a ready Po-ſture for Duty and Service, O, 'tis the Reſtleſneſs and Diſcompoſure of our Hearts that unfits and in-diſpoſes us for our Work and Duty. When the Iſraelites *were filled with Anguiſh of Spirit, they could not hear* Moſes, *Exod.* 6. 9. and when *Jonah* his Spirit was off its Reſt, though he were an Eminent Prophet of God, he could not pray but very pee-viſhly and unbecomingly, *Jon.* 4. 2, 3. A reſt-leſs Spirit is unfit for the ordinary Duties of Chri-ſtianity : But now take a Soul that is indeed at Reſt in God, and he is fit not only for the general Duties of Chriſtianity, ſuch as Prayer, Hearing, or the like, but even for whatever Work or Duty God ſhall call him out unto, though never ſo dif ficult, or never ſo mean : Such an one may in his Place and Station ſay, as I remember, one brings in *David* ſpeaking to God, *Lord,* (ſays he) *if thou wilt make me a Shepherd to keep Sheep, or if thou wilt make me a King to govern thy People, behold, mine Heart is prepared, I am in a ready Poſture for the one or the other.* Oh, what a ſweet Frame is this ? God may alſo call us to what Condition he pleaſes, to a Condition of Fulneſs or of Want, of Proſperity or Affliction, and the like, now what-ever Condition he calls to, the Soul that is at Reſt in him, is ready for it. Does God call him to Sufferings, to take up and bear the Croſs ? He is ready for this Call of God, for he can *rejoyce, yea, glory, in the Croſs,* Rom. 5. 3. *He can ſing in a Pri-ſon,* as *Paul* and *Sylas* did, *Act.* 16. 25. Does God call him to Fulneſs ? *He knows how to abound,* Does
God

God call him to Wants? *He knows how to be abased:* As *Paul* did, *Phil.* 4. 12. Does God call him to Mourning? He is ready for it, for he, and indeed he alone knows how *to weep, as if he wept not:* Does God call him to rejoicing? He is ready for it, for he, and he alone, can *rejoyce as if he rejoyced not,* which is the fittest Posture and Carriage for each Condition, 1 *Cor.* 7. 30. In a Word, he is fit to live, and fit to die; and let me tell you, that is a great Word, yet a true one, he is fit to die, ready in a good Measure for another World; 'tis a great Thing to die, and 'tis a great Attainment to be ready to die; and that that Soul is that is at Rest in God. I scarce know a more desirable Frame and Posture to die in than this of being at Rest in God: Now if it be a Frame of Soul, which thus renders a Man ready for every Call of God to him, surely it must then be an Excellent Frame.

3. To live at Rest in God is a safe Frame and Posture of Soul; a Frame and Posture of Soul, that secures a Man against Danger, and therefore an Excellent Frame. There is no Soul in the World so secure from Danger as he that is at Rest in God; such an one is *set aloft,* (as you have it) *Prov.* 18. 10. *The Name of the Lord is a strong Tower, the Righteous flee thereunto, and are safe,* or, (as the Word is) *are set aloft, set aloft* above the Reach of Danger: They flee to the Name, to the Nature, to the Attributes of God, they retire there, and rest there, and are secured against Danger. This is what guards and fences the Soul, and that against his grand Enemy, the Devil: 'Tis a great and sweet Scripture, that *Phil.* 4. 7. *The Peace of God, which passeth all Understanding, shall keep,* φξεφησει, shall guard or garrison *your Hearts and Minds through Christ Jesus,* it shall fence and fortifie you against Temptation; and indeed no Soul is so fenced and fortified against Temptation, as he

that

that lives at Rest in God : Those Temptations
which wound others, and lead them captive into
Sin, cannot fasten upon him : A true Rest in God
is a kind of Life-guard to the Soul, and no Guard
like it in the World, it keeps Temptation from
entering in, and it keeps Corruption from breaking out. 'Tis a sweet Exposition which one gives
of that Place, *The Peace of God shall keep your
Hearts and Minds, that is* (says he) *that Rest and
Tranquility of Soul which the Faithful have in God,
shall preserve their Hearts as with a Military Guard
and Power, against the Temptations of Satan and the
World, and it shall keep their Minds stable in Christ.*
And to the same Purpose also *Calvin* upon the
Place, *The Peace of God* (says he) *shall keep you,
lest by wicked Thoughts or Desires you shall revolt from
God.* O, my Beloved, there is scarce any thing
gives the Devil and his Temptations greater Ad-
vantage against us, than a disturbed, restless, discomposed, Spirit: So much is evident from *Eph.*
4. 26, 27. *Be ye angry, and sin not, let not the Sun
go down upon your Wrath, neither give Place unto the
Devil.* Where is clearly intimated, that by an unquiet, disturbed, Spirit we give Place unto the Devil, and there is scarce any thing on the other
Hand that so fences and fortifies the Soul against
Satan and his Temptations, as an Holy Rest of
Soul in God. The Saints in Heaven are out of all
Danger, either of Sin or Temptation, and why
so ? Truly for this Reason among others, because
there they are perfectly at Rest in God, they find
that perfect Solace and Satisfaction in God, that they
cannot possibly admit of Sin, nor have they the
least Tendency to turn aside to any thing else.
What shall I say? A Soul that is off his Rest, is off
his Watch, and being off his Watch, he is in the
Mouth of Danger; whereas 'tis quite otherwise
with a Soul at Rest in God.

4. To

4. To live at Reft in God is a very comfortable Frame and Pofture of Soul, which is attended with much Spiritual Comfort and Communion with God, which alfo fpeaks the Excellency of it. A Soul living at Reft in God has ufually the fulleft Comforts, and the fweeteft Communion, with God of any one this fide Heaven · The Truth is, the Thing it felf carries unexpreffible Sweetnefs in it, befides God's Delight to manifeft himfelf to thofe that live in the Exercife of it. God, you know, was in the *ftill Voice*, and there the Prophet found him: *He was not in the great and ftrong Wind, he was not in the Earthquake, he was not in the Fire; but he was in the ftill Voice*, 1 King. 19. 11, 12. The good Prophet had been off his Reft in God; he had been in a Paffion, and under great Difcompofure of Spirit, as you may fee *Verf.* 4. and now God gives him this Vifion of the Wind, the Earthquake, and the Fire, to let him fee that that was not the Way to Communion with him; and fo to caution him againft Paffion and all Difcompofure of Spirit, which he was naturally very prone unto. O, God loves to dwell in, and meet with, a fedate, ferene, compofed, Spirit, a Spirit compofed and at Reft in himfelf, and thofe that are fo, are the Souls who ufually have the cleareft Sights, the fweeteft Taftes, and the fulleft Communications, of Love from him of all others; thofe are they who have the moft clofe and conftant Communion with him, who are moft in his Bofom, and the Embraces of his everlafting Arms; who have moft of his Spirit, his Prefence, his Confolations, given to them: *Acquaint thy felf with God, and be at Peace, fo fhall Good come unto thee,* Job 22. 21. *be at Peace,* to wit, in thine own Spirit, be of a fedate Mind, do not rave, do not rage, do not diftemper and difcompofe thy felf as thou haft done, but be quiet and fedate in thine own Soul: Well, but what fhall I gain by it? Why, *thereby*

thereby Good ſhall come unto thee : And what Good :
Not only outward, temporal, Good, but alſo ſpi-
ritual Good, the Good of Grace, the Good of Divine Conſolations, the Good of Communion with
God, and the ſpecial Manifeſtations of his Love.
O, the more a Man's Soul is at Reſt in God, the
more full will his Comforts, and the more intimate will his Communion with God, be: As for
a reſtleſs, diſturbed, Spirit, 'tis ſo like the Devil,
(as by and by you will hear) that God cannot tell
how to be much with it, nor yet to do much in a
Way of Special Grace and Spiritual Comfort for
it. Chriſtians complain many times, that they
have but little Communion with God, but little
Experience of his Love and Preſence with them;
and one Reaſon, among others, why they have
Cauſe ſo to complain, is, becauſe they are no more
at Reſt in God · Were they more at Reſt in him,
he would reſt more in his Love, his Grace, his
Preſence, with and upon them.

5 To live at Reſt in God is a God-like Frame
and Poſture of Soul, which greatly reſembles God,
and is ſuitable to him, and which brings us up into the very Life and Bleſſedneſs of God himſelf;
and what a choice Frame muſt it then needs be?
The more Likeneſs and Reſemblance any thing
carries in it to God, and the more any thing
brings us into the Life and Bleſſedneſs of God, the
more excellent it is, now there is nothing does
more reſemble God, or is more ſuitable to him,
nothing that brings us more up into the Life and
Likeneſs of God, than to be thus at Reſt in him
in our own Souls, This indeed is the very Life
and Perfection of God, the Poſture (if I may ſo
ſpeak) which God himſelf lives in, for he is ever
at Reſt in himſelf, he is infinitely well pleaſed with
what he himſelf does, and reſts infinitely ſatisfied
with his own Fulneſs and Excellencies : God is his
                                                    own

own Reft, his own Centre ; God is infinitely delighted with his own Will, and infinitely fatisfied
with his own Fulnefs, and fo is at Reft in himfelf,
which indeed is his Bleffednefs : Accordingly the
more our Souls are at Reft in him, the more do
we refemble him, and are brought into his Life
and his Bleffednefs. A reftlefs, unquiet, Spirit does
above all things refemble the Devil, and is fuitable
to the Devil; tis indeed the very Life, Image, and
Spirit, of the Devil; for the Devil is a reftlefs, unquiet, Spirit, always acting in Oppofition to God,
and always fretting at the Difpenfations of God.
He feeks Reft, but finds none, Mat. 12. 43. As Wicked ones cannot reft, fo neither can the Wicked
one reft, but is perpetually difturbed · Now as a
reftlefs, unquiet, Spirit refembles the Devil, and
is the very Life and Image of the Devil, fo to be
at Reft in God is what refembles God, and is the
very Life of God in the Soul ; 'tis what brings us
up into the Divine Life, the Divine Bleffednefs;
and O what an Excellent Frame muft this be ?

6. To live at Reft in God, is a God-honouring
Frame and Pofture of Soul, a Frame of Soul that
does much honour God, and give Glory to him ;
and therefore muft have much Worth and Excellency in it. Of all Frames, as well as Actions,
that is the beft that does honour and glorifie God
moft, and what Frame of Soul does more honour
and glorifie God than this of being at Reft in him ?
This gives to God the Glory of his Sovereignty,
and the Glory of his Sufficiency, Two of the
brighteft Jewels in the Crown of Heaven : It owns
and acknowledges God to be both beft and greateft, the higheft Lord, and the chiefeft Good, and
fo it glorifies God as God, it fets him up as God
in the Soul, and gives him the Honour due unto
his Name as fuch. Reftlefs, difturbed, unquiet,
Spirits do darken and obfcure the Glory of God;
they

they are *Censores Divinitatis*, (as one of the Anti-
ents speaks of them) they censure the Blessed
God, and do in effect deny and disown the So
vereignty of God, the Wisdom of God, the Good
ness, the Faithfulness, of God, the Fulness, Sufficiency, and Perfection, of the Holy One, they do
in effect say that God's Will is not a Good, a Wise,
and an Holy, Will, that there is not enough in
God to satisfie Souls, and make them happy ; and
O what an Affront and Dishonour is this to the
Majesty of Heaven ? But now the Soul that is indeed at Rest in God, he gives him the Glory of
all, he sets the Crown where it ought to be, and
Oh how much does this speak out the Worth and
Excellency of this Frame of Soul?

7. To live at Rest in God, is an Honoured and
Highly Esteemed Frame and Posture of Soul, and
that by God himself, a Frame and Posture of Soul,
which God has a great Honour for, and puts a
great Value upon, which also speaks the Excellen
cy of it : There is scarce any Frame of Soul that
God more values, honours, and delights in, than
this of an Holy Rest in himself : This is *in the Sight
of God of great Price : Put on the Ornament of a
meek and quiet Spirit, which in the Sight of God is
of great Price :* 1 *Pet.* 3. 4 In the Sight of Men,
at least unholy and unspiritual Men, 'tis of little
Price, of no Price, they despise and contemn it,
but God has other Thoughts and other Values of
it, he highly esteems and honours it, he looks on
it as one of the choicest Ornaments, as one of the
highest Excellencies of any Soul ; now certainly
that is best which God values and honours most.
As that which honours God most, so that which
God most honours, must have most of true Worth
and Excellency in it. A restless, unquiet, Spirit
on the one Hand, or a Spirit at Rest in the Crea
ture on the other Hand, is what God abhors and
despises

despises; but a Spirit at Rest in himself he highly values.

8. To live at Rest in God is a Heavenly Frame and Posture of Soul, a Frame and Posture of Soul which carries much of Heaven in it; 'tis indeed in a great Measure the Life of Heaven here on Earth; and what then more Excellent than this? Pray, my Beloved, what is Heaven, and the Life of Heaven, the Life which the Saints and Angels liv in Heaven? Heaven is a State of *Rest,* Heb. 4. 9. and what is that Rest? True, there is an external Rest, there is a Rest from Labour and Trouble, from Conflict and Temptation; but the main of it is the inward Rest of the Soul, that Rest and Complacency which the Soul enjoys in God, and shall enjoy in him and with him for ever. There the Soul is filled with God, he is perfectly swallowed up in the Divine Will, being thorowly conformed thereunto, and he has the Perfect Vision and Fruition of the Divine Glory and Fulness, *seeing him as he is,* 1 *Joh.* 3. 2. And in both these he is filled with even an infinite Content and Satisfaction of Heart, this is the True Rest of Heaven. And what is the Life which the Saints and Angels live there? 'Tis a Life of perfect Rest and Solace in God, such Rest and Solace in God, as that they never think of going out to any thing else whatever. *God is all in all to them,* 1 *Cor.* 15 28. Thus to be at Rest in God is an Heavenly Frame and Posture of Soul; and Oh what an Excellent Frame must this be? Well then, Lay all these Eight Things together, and you shall find an incomparable Worth and Excellency in it, which is a further Evidence of the Saint's Duty and Interest to live therein.

G   C H A P.

CHAP. V.

The Truth particularly improved. The Saints called upon to live thus at Rest in God. Arguments urged to induce them so to do.

WHat it is for the Soul to be at Rest in God, what Obligations the Saints are under to live at Rest in him, the Excellency of this Frame and Posture of Spirit, you have seen laid open before you, now what shall we say to these Things? O, that all who profess themselves to be Saints, or would be accounted so, would give all Diligence always to live thus at Rest in God. Possibly some of us are quite off our Centre, our Souls are full of Storms and Tempests, Tossings and Tumblings, they are not only *cast down*, but also *disquieted within us*, (as Holy *David's* sometimes was) *Psal.* 42. 11. Others of us perhaps are at Rest, but 'tis a sinful Rest, at Rest in the Creature, and not in God, at Rest in carnal, sensible, Things, we are of those who *are at Ease in* Zion , yea, perhaps we are even singing that mad *Requiem* to our Soul's, that that Fool sometimes did, *Luke* 12. 19. *Soul, take thine Ease, eat, drink, and be merry, thou hast Goods laid up for thee for many Years* · But now this Truth, and the Things declared about it, do call upon the one and the other of us to return to God as our Rest, and to centre purely and entirely in him alone · This Truth calls off the one from all those unquiet Motions and Agitations that are within us, from all our Tossings and Tumblings, to an Holy Calm and Quiet of Heart in God; as it calls off the other from all our false Rests and Reposes, to an Holy Rest and Repose in God; and Oh that both the one and the other would hear and obey this Call, taking up our Rest in God alone. O, my Beloved! Are you under such Obligations to live at Rest in God as you are ? And

yet

yet will you not live at Reft in him? On the other
Hand, is the Frame and Pofture of Soul fo Excellent? And will you negleft it, and not ftudy to be
found always therein? Let me recapitulate a little
particularly: Has God freely made over himfelf
in all his Fulnefs and Riches, in his Covenant, to
you, as your Reft and Portion for ever, and yet
will you not live at Reft in him? Have you chofen
God, and voucht him for your God and Portion,
and yet will you not live at Reft in him? Is God
fo much (as you have heard) at Reft in you, and
yet will you not live at Reft in him? Shall you,
and do you, hope to live at Reft in God, and with
God, for ever in Heaven, and yet will you not
live at Reft in him here? O methinks thefe things
fhould conftrain you. On the other Hand, fhould
not the Excellency of the Frame allure you?
Would you live forth much of the Life and Power
of Grace? Then live at Reft in God. Would you
be ready for every Call of God to you, whether to
do or to fuffer, to live or to die? Then live at Reft
in God. Would you be fenced and fortified againft
Temptation? Then live at Reft in God. Would
you enjoy much Spiritual Comfort and Communion with God? Then live at Reft in God. Would
you be like God? Would you refemble God, and
grow up into his Life and Bleffednefs? Then live
at Reft in God. Would you honour God? You
have greatly difhonoured him, would you now
honour him? Then live at Reft in him. Would
you live in Heaven, and begin the Life of Heaven
here on Earth? Then live at Reft in God. O
why fhould we think of any other Reft but God?
Or why fhould we live in any other Pofture of
Soul but this of a Reft in him? Is there any fo
fweet, fo amiable, fo becoming, as this? Oh let
us labour, as near as poffible, always to be found
in this Pofture. Bleffed be God that we may reft
in him: Two Things we fhould blefs God for:

one is, that there is a Rest remaining for us in the other World, whether we find Rest here or no, yet there is a Rest to come, a Blessed Rest, *Heb.* 4. 9. The other is, that there is a Rest in God for us, and that we may enter into, and live in, that Rest even here; when there is no Rest to be had in this World's Enjoyments, no Rest in or from the Creature, yet then there is a Rest to be had in God, and from God, *We that have believed do enter into Rest, Heb.* 4. 3. there is a Rest in God, in the Will, the Presence, the Love, the Fulness of God, which we do or may enter into, even here in this World; and Blessed be God for this Rest, and this is the Rest which I am now calling you into. And yet a little further, to set home the Call upon you, consider a few Things.

1. Consider what a sad and dismal thing it is for a Soul to rest in any thing but God alone. A Rest, one or another, the Soul will have: If God be not its Rest, it will be taking up a Rest elsewhere: Now 'tis a sad and woful thing for a Soul to rest any where but in God alone. *Woe to them that are at Ease in Zion,* (says the Prophet) *Amos* 6. 1. Woe to them that are Quiet and at Rest in *Zion*; that is to say, that are at Rest in carnal sensual Things in *Zion*; so the Prophet afterwards explains himself; Woe to them that are at Rest in the Creatures, that take up their Solace and Satisfaction in Carnal Contentments, and not in God. To take up our Rest in the Creatures, and not in God, is for us to prefer the Creature before God, and to be content with the Creature without God, for our Portion and Happiness for ever: And, which is more, 'tis a dreadful Argument that a Man's All lyes in the Creature, and that God intends him nothing but the Creature for ever. *Woe unto you that are Rich,* (says Christ) *for you have received your Consolation,* Luke 6. 24. *Woe unto you that are Rich,* that is, *you who rest in your Riches,* (as

Calvin

Calvin rightly expounds it) *who take up your Happiness in these things. Woe unto you :* And what Woe to them ? Truly a most dreadful Woe ; *You have received your Consolation,* (says Christ) you have all the Good you are ever like to have, you shall have no more and no other Happiness or Consolation for ever: Your resting in these Things argues these Things to be your All ; and Oh, what a woful, dreadful, thing is it for a Man to have his All in this World, in a few, vain, empty, bitter, sweet, perishing, Vanities here ! 'Twas a cutting, killing, Word which *Abraham* is brought in giving *Dives,* when he said, *Son, remember that thou in thy Life-time receivedst thy good things,* Luke 16. 25. He had all his Happiness in this World, which is the Woe and Misery of such as take up their Rest anywhere but in God alone: Tremble therefore at this.

2. Consider how impossible it is to find any true Rest, Solace, and Satisfaction, of Soul anywhere but in God and with God alone. You may as soon find Life in Death, or Light in Darkness, as Rest for your Souls anywhere but in God alone. ————Pray, Friends, where will you look, or whither will you go, to find Rest on this side God and Christ ? Will you have Recourse to Sin ? To your Lusts ? To these Multitudes run; they pursue their Rest, Solace, and Satisfaction, from Sin, and the Pleasures of Sin ; yea, (as *Solomon* speaks) *they rest not unless they sin,* unless they do evil: But, my Beloved, is there Rest to be found in Sin ? Can that give Rest that is the greatest Evil in the World ? Can that give Rest that is the Cause of all our Troubles and Difficulties ? Can that give Rest that is the Cause of all the Confusions and Desolations that are in the World ? Can that give Rest that was the first and only Cause and Founder of Hell? Had there been no Sin, there had been no

G 3   Hell.

Hell. Can that give Rest that makes us like the Devil, that restless Spirit; yea, and that made him of a Glorious Angel a Devil? Can that give Rest that is infinitely contrary to God, that is the only Object of his Hatred, and that alone can and does separate between God, the chief Good, and our Souls? O, the Folly of Souls to pursue a Rest in Sin, in the Satisfaction of a Lust! True, a base, brutish, Pleasure and Delight wicked Men take in Sin, (as he said) *Will it not be Bitterness in the latter End?* *The Wages of Sin is Death,* Rom. 6 ult. Yea, and not only Death at last, but many times Anguish and Torment here. Will you have Recourse to the good Things of this World, to Creature Comforts and Enjoyments, to Friends, Relations, Estate, and the like? These Thousands make their Rest practically, saying with him, *Luke* 12. 19. *Soul, take thine Ease, thou hast Goods laid up for thee for many Years.* Thou hast a good Trade, a fair Estate, pleasant Enjoyments, *take thine Ease, Soul,* sit thou down at Rest. But, my Beloved, can these Things give Rest? Alas! 'tis the joint Language of all the Creatures to us, Rest and Happiness for your Souls is not to be found in us, seek it elsewhere if you intend to find it. *The Creatures* (says a Worthy Divine) *are not good, at least they are not the Soul's Good,* nothing (says he) *but an infinite Godhead can allay your Hunger after Happiness.* Can Wind, can Vanity, can a Shadow, can a Fancy, can Things of Nought, Things that are not, Things that are even made up of Emptiness and Changeableness, give Rest? Such (you know) these Things are in Scripture represented to be. Could these Things have given Rest why had not *Solomon* found it in them? He had certainly the fullest Enjoyment of them that ever Man had, and not only so, but moreover he had Wisdom and Skill to extract the Sweetness of them, to improve
whatever

whatever they have in them, yea, and he improved this Wisdom and Skil of his to the utmost, for he set himself (as he tells us) to enjoy whatever the Creature could possibly afford, he gave himself up to a full Enjoyment of all Well, but did he find Rest in them after all? No, he was so far from finding Rest, that he cries out of all, *All is Vanity and Vexation of Spirit*, and this he does often, (you know) *All is Vanity and Vexation of Spirit*, and can *Vanity and Vexation of Spirit* give Rest? What if a Man has an Affluence, an Abundance of these Things, and they are also increasing daily, will they not afford a Rest for him then? No, *he that loveth Silver shall not be satisfied with Silver, nor he that loveth Abundance with Increase, this also is Vanity, Eccles.* 5. 10. Silver, Abundance, Increase, all is Vanity, and cannot give Rest. And, my Beloved, does not our Experience tell us the same Thing? Alas, did we ever find any true Rest and Satisfaction of Soul in these Things? True, we are apt to promise our selves Rest in this and that, in this Condition, and that Enjoyment, but did we ever find that which we promised our selves? Have we not always met with Disappointments? We have dreamed of a Rest in these Things, but it has been but a Dream It has been with us as 'tis in the Prophet *Isa.* 29. 8. *It shall be as when a hungry Man dreameth, and behold he eateth, but he awaketh, and his Soul is empty, or, as when a thirsty Man dreameth, and behold he drinketh, but he awaketh, and behold he is faint, and his Soul hath Appetite.* Just so 'tis, and it has been, with us, while we are or have been pursuing Rest, and promising our selves Rest in and from the Creature Yea, and others of the Saints have experienced and asserted the same thing, *All things* (says *Aug.*) *are full of Trouble and Difficulty, thou alone, O God, art the true Rest.* And 'tis a great Speech of his, wor-

thy

thy to be written upon the Table of our Hearts,
speaking to Souls who are gone off from God:
Return, ye Prevaricators, (says he) *to your selves,
and cleave unto him that made you, stand with him,
and ye shall stand, rest in him, and ye shall rest.* And
again, says he, *Rest and Happiness is not to be found
where you seek it, seek what you seek, but know that
'tis not to be found where you seek it. You seek a Blessed Life in the Region of Death, and 'tis not there, for
how should a Blessed Life be found there where there
is not so much as Life it self?* The Sum of all seems
to be this, That those that desert God do go from
the true Rest and Happiness of Souls, and to seek
Rest and Happiness any where but in God and
Christ, is to seek the Living among the Dead.
Once more, will you have Recourse to your selves,
and be your own Rest? Indeed we read that *a
good Man shall be satisfied from himself,* Prov. 14. 14.
but how *from himself? From himself* in Union and
Communion with his God. *From himself* as in
Communion with him that is the Chief Good,
that has all Good in him, and not otherwise: And
therefore observe, *the Good Man* here stands in Op-
position to the *Backslider,* one that is gone off
from God: Our selves, considered abstractly in
themselves, are most insufficient to give Rest to
the Soul, being most vain, changeable and deceitful *Every Man in his best State is altogether Vanity,* Psal. 39. 5. 'Tis a great saying I have read
in *Bern. I have sought Rest* (says he) *in all things
that are seen, but I could not find Rest in them; then
returning to my self, I found I could not possibly subsist
in my self, because my Mind is most light and vain.* In
nothing without, in nothing within, could he find
any Rest, but in God alone. I'll close this Argument with a weighty Speech which I have read
in a Worthy Divine of our own, Blessed Mr. *Bur-
roughs,* who speaking of God's being the Rest and

                                                    Portion

Portion of his People, fpeaks thus: 'Suppofe
'(fays he) that God fhould caufe all the Kings and
'Emperors in the World to come and caft down
'their Crowns at the Foot of an Holy Soul, and
'fay, All thefe are thine; he would anfwer, This
'is not enough, for this is not God himfelf: Sup-
'pofe God fhould bring all the Splendors of all
'the Creatures in Heaven and Earth, and they
'fhould be caft at the Foot of an Holy Soul 'as
'his, he would fay, This is not enough, this
'is not God himfelf: Suppofe God fhould
'caufe all the Glory of Heaven, not only of
'Sun, Moon, and Stars, but alfo of the higheft
'Heaven, abftracted from God, to be laid before
'an Holy Soul as his, he would fay, This is not
'enough, this is not God himfelf. Once more,
'fhould all the Angels come, and fay to an Holy
'Soul, We are fent to put all our Glory upon thee;
'he would fay, This is not enough, for this is not
'God himfelf. O, nothing but God in Chrift can
'give Reft to Souls.

3. Confider what a Bleffed Reft God is for Souls,
or that Souls may find in God. As there is an utter Impoffibility of finding Reft anywhere but in
God; fo in him there is a Bleffed Reft to be found
for Souls, a full, a perfect, an eternal, Reft. O,
my Beloved, what can your Souls defire, or what
are they capable of, that is not to be found in God?
Would you have Good? It muft be Good that can
give Reft to the Soul: God is Good, he is the
Chief Good, the Beft, the Higheft, Good; he is
Goodnefs it felf, he is Good in himfelf, and he
is the Spring and Fountain of all that Good that is
in the Creature: He is fo Good as that he is the
Good of all Good; and nothing has any thing of
Goodnefs in it, but as it refembles him, and parti-
cipates of him. *There is none Good but One, that is
God*, Mat. 19. 17. *He is God that made me*, (fays
Aug.) *and he is my Good, and in him do I exult and*

rejoice before all my other good Things whatsoever, and in all my other good Things. Would you have a full Good? Such a God is God, there is a Fulness of all Good in him, *He that overcometh shall inherit all Things: How so? I will be his God.* I'll be his, and in having me he will have all in me, *Rev.* 21. 7. Whatever Good, Beauty, or Excellency, there is in the Creature, yea, in all the Creatures put together, 'tis all but a small Drop or Ray to that Good, Beauty, and Excellency, that is in God: 'Tis but a small Spark to the Ocean of the Divine Goodness. *Lord, (says Austin) all those Things which thou hast made are beautiful, but thou thy self art infinitely more beautiful.* God has all Kinds and all Degrees of Good in him: He is Light, and Life, and Love, and Peace, and Joy, and Holiness, and Salvation, and what not that God is, or that conduces to the Happiness of Eternal Souls? *Thou, Lord, art that Good, where no Good is wanting, (says Aug.) and thou art always at Rest, because thou art thine own Rest.* That little Good that is found in the Creature is narrow, scanty; and but here and there a Drop. But God has all Good in a Blessed Union and Conjunction in him. O how Glorious a Rest may the Soul find in him! ——Would you have a suitable and convenient Good? Such a Good is God, he is a suitable and convenient Good, a Good suitable to the Nature, Life, and Wants, of the Soul: Among all your Creature Injoyments and Contentments there is nothing suitable either to the Nature or Life of the Soul. They are carnal, sensible, Things, and so are suitable to the Flesh and sensual Part, and are pleasing to it, but they have nothing suitable in them to an immortal Spirit, nothing that an eternal Soul can feed upon. The Body may as soon feed upon Air and Ashes, as the Soul upon Creatures. But now in God there is that Good that is every way suitable to the Soul, to the Nature.

Nature, Life, and Wants, of the Soul: The Soul is of a Spiritual Nature, and God is of a Spiritual Good, *God is a Spirit, Joh* 4. 24. The Soul is of a vast Capacity, 'tis next to Infiniteness in its Capacity and Desires, and God is a vast and comprehensive Good, having (as has been shewn) all Good in him. Without Suitableness in the Object to the Faculty there can be no Rest. ——Would you have an original, independant, Good? Such a Good is God: *Waters drink most pleasantly at the Fountain head*. In God you have all Good, all Sweet, all Comfort, at the Fountain head. Hence he is said to be *a Fountain of Living Waters*, and the Creatures *broken Cisterns, Jer.* 2. 13. the Fountain has all in and from it self, but Cisterns, you know, have no more than is put into them, all that Good that is in God he has it in and from himself; but the Creatures, yea, the best of Creatures, Angels themselves not excepted, have no more than he puts into them. Now how much is the Fountain to be preferred before a Cistern?——Would you have a pure and an unmixed Good, Gold that has no Dross, Wine that has no Water, in it? Such a Good is God. *God is Light, and in him there is no Darkness at all,* 1 *Joh.* 1. 5. All Things on this side God have their Mixtures, they have a dark as well as a bright Side, all this Wine is mixt with Wormwood, this Gold with Dross: Who of us did ever meet with the Creature Injoyment that had not many Allays? The sweetest Rose has its Prickles, and the rarest Beauty its Spots among the Creatures, but now God is every way a pure and an unmixed Good, he is all Light, Life, Love, Holiness, and the like.——Would you have a sweet and satisfying Good? Such a Good is God, yea, indeed there is infinite Sweetness and Satisfaction to be found in him, he can infinitely delight, ravish, solace, and satisfie, the Soul for ever. O how sweet, how satisfying, are

the

the Sights of God, the Tastes and Descents of his
Love! What an Heaven does one Sight of God,
one Descent of his Love, make in the Soul! *David* casting his Eye upon God, as his in Covenant,
is even ravished with it, and cries out, *The Lines
are fallen to me in pleasant Places, I have a goodly
Heritage,* Psal. 16. 5, 6. and elsewhere we read of
Pleasures, of *Rivers of Pleasures,* of *Satisfaction,* of
Abundance of Satisfaction, and all, as that which
Souls do or may find in God, and Communion
with God, *Psal.* 36. 8. and *David* over and over
tells you of *Sweetness,* and *Satisfaction,* and *Satisfaction* as *with Marrow and Fatness* in but the very
Thoughts and Meditation of God, *Psal.* 63. 5, 6.
and *Aug.* (I remember) speaking of God, and to
him, often breaks out into such Language as this,
O, my God, my Life, my Sweetness ! O, Sirs! Ho-
ly Souls, who live in Communion with God, will
tell you, that there is no Sweetness like that in
God, no Love like his Love, no Comforts like his
Comforts: They will tell you, that one Sight of
God, one sensible Token of his Presence in the
Soul, has more Solace and Sweetness in it than all
the Delights of this World; yea, than many
Worlds; and they accordingly chuse and desire it.
Oh how sweet is it to be led into the Banqueting-
House by Christ, and there have the Banner of his
Love displayed over us, and Flaggons of that Wine
poured out unto us! How sweet is it to have one
Sight of the King in his Beauty? How much more to
walk and converse with him in his Galleries? How
sweet is it with God in his Sanctuary, and have
him revealing Himself, his Love, his Beauty, his
Glory, to us? *O taste and see how good the Lord is !*
Would you have a sure, eternal, and unchangea-
ble, Good, a Good that never fades, fails, nor has
any Period? Such a Good is God, and God alone:
From Everlasting to Everlasting he is God, Psal. 90. 2.
But thus has been sufficiently spoken to elsewhere,

Well.

Well, you fee what a Bleffed Reft God is for Souls.
Why then fhould we ever think of looking out anywhere elfe for Reft? O wretched Hearts of ours,
that will leave this God, and go out to a vain
World and dying Creatures for Reft and Happinefs!
In a Word, if God has all that in him which thou
needeft, or art capable of, to give thee Reft and
Happinefs, then retire folely to him for it. Now
what doft thou want? Or what art thou capable
of to give thee Reft and Happinefs? Doft thou
want and defire Life? *With God is the Fountain of
Life, Pfal. 36. 9.* Doft thou want Peace? God is
the God of Peace, Rom. 16. 20. and frequently elfewhere is he fo called. Doft thou want Pardon?
He is the God of Pardon, fo the Words are in
the *Pfalms,* when he is faid *to be ready to forgive.*
And you know he has promifed to *pardon Iniquity,
Tranfgreffion, and Sin,* Sins of all Sorts and Sizes,
all Degrees and Aggravations, if Souls come to
him, *Heb. 8. 12.* Doft thou want Grace? He is
the God of all Grace, 1 *Pet.* 5. 10. Doft thou want
Comfort? He is *the God of all Confolation.* Doft
thou want Mercy? He is *the Father of Mercies,*
2 *Cor.* 1. 3. Doft thou want Strength? Strength
to do, to fuffer, to live, to die? He is *the Lord
Jehovah, with whom is everlafting Strength, Ifa.* 26. 4.
Doft thou want Joy? *In his Prefence is Fulnefs of Joy,
Pfal.* 16. 11. Doft thou want Salvation? Salvation
Temporal, Salvation Eternal? He is *the God of Salvation,* and as fuch the Church glories in him, *Pfal.*
68. 20. Thus no Reft like that in God, Souls need
not look elfewhere for Reft and Happinefs, for
there is all in God alone.

4. Confider what a reftlefs World you live in,
and what a troublefom Time you are fallen upon.
The more reftlefs this World is, and the more
troublefom the Times are which we are fallen upon, the more we are concerned to take up our
Reft in God: Now certainly the World was fcarce
ever more reftlefs, nor the Times more trouble

son, than now. In *Zech* 1. 11. we read of a
Time when the whole World was at Rest, except-
ing only the Church of God ; but 'tis even quite
contrary now, for now the whole World, Church,
and all, are in a restless, troublesom, State. We
fee and hear of little but *Wars, and Rumours of
Wars*, and as 'twas of old, *Destruction upon Destruction is cried*, and what and when the End of
of these Things will be, who can tell ? In *Jer.* 16
5. we read that God had taken away his Peace
from that People, *I have taken away my Peace from
this People, saith the Lord*, and truly now he seems
to have taken away his Peace from the World. I'll
leave only Two Scriptures with you, ore out of
the Old, and the other out of the New, Testa-
ment, both which I am apt to think may have a
great Aspect to the present Days, and may in a
great Measure receive their Accomplishment in
them. One is, *Zeph* 3 8. *Wait ye upon me, saith
the Lord, until the Day that I arise up to the Prey,
for my Determination is to gather the Nations, that I
may assemble the Kingdoms, to pour out upon them mine
Indignation, even all my fierce Anger, for all the
Earth shall be devoured with the Fire of my Jealousie*.
The other is that, *Luke* 21. 25, 26. *There shall be
Signs in the Sun, and in the Moon, and in the Stars,
(and these we have had) and upon the Earth Distress
of Nations, with Perplexity, the Sea and the Waves
roaring, Mens Hearts failing them for Fear, and for
looking after those Things which are coming on the
Earth, for the Powers of Heaven shall be shaken*. I say
nothing, only I fear, as we have seen some
of these Things accomplisht, so there will be a more
full Accomplishment of them, and that e'er the
present Generation passes away. Doubtless great
Storms are a coming, and happy they that have
an Ark to hide themselves in, God has now great
Works to do, he has the Kingdom of Antichrist
utterly to destroy, the *Kingdom* of his Son Christ
                                                        to

to fet up in its Luftre and Glory, the final Redemption of his People to work out, his ancient Ones to call in, and his fuffering Name, Attributes, and Glory, fully to right and Vindicate, and thefe Things are not like to be brought about without great S-orms, Convulfions, and Concuffions, in the World: Well, and what is the Language of all this to us? Verily this, Souls recive into God, take up your Reft in him, make him your All, both here and in Eternity And Oh that we would do fo! Then fhould we reft in the Day of Trouble. When *Noah* forefaw the Deluge a coming, *he prepared him an Ark to the faving of both himfelf and Family, Heb.* 11 7. Surely he is blind indeed that does not fee a Deluge coming upon the World, a Deluge of outward Troubles and Calamities. O why do we not enark in God, by making him our Reft. This God invites his People unto, *Ifa.* 26. 20. *Come, my People, enter thou into thy Chambers, and fhut thy Doors about thee, hide thy felf, as it were, for a little Moment, until the Indignation be over-paft: For, behold, the Lord cometh out of his Place to punifh the Inhabitants of the Earth for their Iniquity.* What is it for God's People to enter into their Chambers, and hide themfelves, but to retire more into him, live at Reft and in Communion with him, to put themfelves under his Protection, and the like? 'Tis for them to retire from the World and worldly Concerns, and to make him All, living and refting wholly in him, and upon him. O let this, *viz* the Reftlefnefs of the World you live in, draw your Souls into an Holy Reft in God.

5. Confider what Enemies you are to your own Souls, by not living at Reft in God. He *that finneth*, ('tis faid) *wrongeth his own Soul*, he that lives not at Reft in God, greatly finneth, and thereby greatly wrongeth his own Soul. On the one Hand, you hereby deprive your Souls of much Good;

Good; and on the other Hand you expofe your Souls to much Evil.

1. Hereby you deprive your Souls of much Good, yea, of much of the beft Good. *Solomon* found this in Experience, and tells us, that purfuing Reft and Happinefs in the Creature, and not in God, he did thereby *bereave his Soul of Good, Ecclef.* 4. 8. and what Good ? Verily the beft Good, the Good of Grace, of Holinefs, of Communion with God, of the Comforts of his Spirit, and the like: And Oh how much of this Good do you bereave your Souls of daily? This is that which hath bereaved you of much Grace, much Love, much Spiritual Comfort, many Embraces in the Arms and Bofom of Chrift's Love: This (namely our purfuing Reft from the Creature, and not living at Reft in God) is that which hath made us fo lean, fo dead, fo dry, fo barren in our Spirits, as we are. O, my Beloved, while we have been off our Reft in God, and have taken up in other Things, what have we been doing, but feeding upon Husks and Swill, when we might have eaten Bread, and drunk Wine, in the Father's Kingdom? What have we been doing, but following after lying Vanities, to the forfaking of our own Mercies? Oh, did you know how fweet a Life it is to be at Reft in God, you would then know what Good you have bereaved your Souls of, by not living at Reft in him.

2. Hereby you expofe your Souls to much Evil. I remember a Saying of *Auftin, In this I finned,* (fays he) *that I fought my Happinefs not in God, but in his Creatures, and fo I rufht upon all manner of Dolours, Confufions, and Errors, of Soul :* And have not we done fo ? O the Wounds, the Confufions, the Errors, of Soul, which we have expofed our felves unto, while we have been off our Reft in God! Sin and Satan have made great Wafte and Defolation upon our Spirits : And 'tis what expofes us to nothing but Sorrows, Snares, and Death : And

And as we would not wrong our Souls, let us retire to, and live at, Reſt in God.

6. Conſider that your living at Reſt in God here
will be a clear and unqueſtionable Evidence to you,
that you ſhall live at Reſt in God and with God
for ever. O how ſweet is it to have any one clear
Evidence of living at Reſt in God and with God in
Heaven? And what would ſome of our Souls at
ſome times give for ſuch a Bleſſing? Yea, how
ſweet is a ſmall Glimpſe of Hope, a ſecret Whiſ-
per, an inward Hint or Intimation, of ſuch a thing
from the Spirit of God in our Souls? O, live at
Reſt in God here, and this will be a broad Evidence of it to you, and truly, unleſs you do live at
Reſt in him here, I know not how ever you will
make it out to your Souls that you ſhall live at
Reſt in him and with him in the other World. In
ſhort, my Beloved, if we do indeed deſire to live
at Reſt with God for ever in Heaven, why ſhould
we not deſire to live at Reſt in God here? Sure I am,
the Thing is the ſame, and we ſhou'd deſire the
one as well as the other, and the one as the Evidence of the other. O, come, come, and be pre-
vailed with by theſe Things, one and all, to take up
the Reſt of your Souls purely and ſolely in God!

CHAP. VI.

Several plain and proper Directions to Souls how to at-
tain unto this Life of a Reſt in God. With a Con-
cluſion of the whole Matter.

TO live at Reſt in God, that is a ſweet, a bleſſed,
Life indeed; but how may we attain to it?
Our Souls would be at it, but how may we come
up hereunto? A few Directions in that Caſe, and
I'll cloſe all.

1. Would you indeed live at Reſt in God? Then
deſpair of ever finding Reſt anywhere but in him
alone.

alone. As long as we have any Hopes of a Reft
any where elfe, we will not fo purely take up our
Reft in God as we fhould , for woe and alas for us!
Our *Heart is bent to back fliding from him*, Hof. 11. 7.
We are carnal and fenfual, and are addicted to
carnal and fenfual Things . As ever therefore you
would live at Reft in God, utterly defpair in your
felves of ever finding Reft , yea, any thing of
Reft anywhere elfe   The more we are driven out
of the Creature, cut of all our falfe Refts and Re-
pofes, the nearer we are to an Holy Reft and Re-
pofe in God : It has been fufficiently evidenced
and declared, that there is no true Reft for a Soul
but in God alone, and you have both feen and
heard it , but, my Beloved, 't s one thing to hear
this by the hearing of the Ear, and another thing
for the Soul to come under the Senfe and Power
thereof, fo as indeed to be dead in our Hopes to
all other things, and practically to defpair of Reft
and Happinefs anywhere but in God alone. Whatever we pretend or profefs, at leaft the moft of us,
we ftill think that there is fome Reft, fome Happinefs, in fomewhat elfe befides God, and fhort of
God , elfe what mean our eager Defires after other
things, our Delights in them when enjoyed, our
Grief and Sorrow of Heart when loft or wanting?
What means the Secret Bent and Byas of our Heart
to ftand off from God, and cleave to other Things,
and the like? But all this muft be rooted out,
firmly fixing this Foundation Principle in your
Souls, that there is no Reft for a Soul but in God
alone, and accordingly never have a Thought of
looking elfewhere. And when at any time the Heart
wou'd be going out to other Things, check it with
this Confideration, Reft, for the Soul is to be
found only in God.

2. Would you indeed live at Reft in God? Then
labour to know him much, and to know him in
Chrift,

Chrift. The more we know God, the more we fhall love him; and the more we know and love him, the more fhall we reft in him: *They that know thy Name* (fays the *Pfalmift*) *will truft in thee, Pfal.* 9. 10. they will reft in thee, depend on thee: One great Reafon why we do not reft in God, is, becaufe we do not know him, at leaft fo know him as to carry in us right Notions and Apprehenfions of him: Labour therefore to know God more and better, labour to know him in Chrift: God in Chrift is moft fweet, moft lovely, moft ravifhing and folicing, to Souls, God in Chrift is a God of Love, yea, a God that is Love *God is Love,* (fays St. *John*) 1 *Joh.* 4 8. God in Chrift is a God of Reconciliation, *God was in Chrift reconciling the World unto himfelf, not imputing their Trefpaffes to them,* 2 *Cor.* 5. 19, 20. and Oh how fweet is God thus known! God in Chrift is *the Father of Mercies, the God of all Grace and Comfort,* 2 *Cor.* 1. 3. he is a full, free, open, Fountain of all Spiritual Good. In 2 *Cor* 4. 6. we read of *the Light of the Knowledge of the Glory of God fhining forth in the Face of Chrift :* And indeed the Light and Glory of God, his Beauty, Sweetnefs, and Excellency, fhines forth nowhere fo Brightly and Illuftrioufly as in Jefus Chrift. To know God, or to look on him out of Chrift, is what rather fills the Soul with Trouble, than brings it to Reft in him. *I remembred God, and was troubled,* (faid he) *Pfal.* 77. 3. God out of Chrift is no other than an angry Judge, a confuming Fire, one that is ready to damn and deftroy the Soul , but in Chrift he is a God of Pardon, a God of Salvation, to all that come by Chrift to him. Hence fome of the Saints have profeft that they durft not think of God out of Chrift And (you know) what *Luther's* Thoughts were by that Outcry of his , *I'll have nothing to do with an Abfolute God.* O therefore labour to know

know God in Chrift more ; being known in him, he is infinitely fweet to Souls, and they cannot but find that Sweetn fs in him that fhall draw and allure them to make him their Reft and All for ever.

3. Would you indeed live at Reft in God? Then labour to get your Covenant-Intereft in, and Relation to, God cleared up to you. The clearer your Intereft in God is to you, the fuller and more conftant will your Reft in him be ; and indeed you will never fo fully and fweetly acquiefce in God as you fhould, until you come to fome good Senfe of your Intereft in him, and Relation to him in Chrift and the Covenant: In 1 *Sam.* 30. 6. 'tis faid, that *David encouraged his Heart in the Lord* [*his God ;*] he faw God to be [his God,] and feeing him to be fo, he encouraged himfelf in him, he fat down fatisfied and at Reft in him, and that in the midft of many, great, and fore, Diftreffes, as you may there fee : Had he not feen him to be his, I queftion whether he would have been able to fit down at Reft in him, as he did, efpecially in fo great a Storm ? So the Church, Lam. 3. 24. *The Lord is my Portion, faith my Soul, therefore I'll hope in him :* Seeing God to be her Portion, fhe could hope, truft, reft, in him, and that in a Cafe of great Calamity and Diftrefs. I will not fay a Soul cannot Reft in God without a Senfe of his Intereft in him ; no, 'tis the Soul's Duty to reft in God however things go with him, though he be *in the Dark,* though God has withdrawn himfelf from the Soul, yet *the Soul fhould truft in the Name of the Lord, and reft himfelf in his God,* Ifa. 50. 10. ftill there is that in God that is a full and proper Matter or Ground of Reft in him, for he is as High, as Holy, as Wife, as Good, as All-fufficient, as ever he was, and indeed we fhould learn to believe in the Dark : But though this be fo, yet

ftill

ftill I fay, the clea er y in Intc.eft in God is to you, the more fully as fweer y will you reft in him. The Senfe of an inte en't od is what is moft effectual to reduce a S u o in Reft in God, when through Temptation it has been carried off from it: So we find, *Pfal* 42. 11. (which may be further opened afterwards) as ever therefore you would live purely and entirely at Reft in God, get your Intereft in him, as your God and Father, cleared up to you; firft chufe him for your God and Portion; and do it every Day, never reft till you can fay, *Lord, whom have I in Heaven but thee? And there is none upon Earth that I defire befides thee: My Heart and my Flefh fail, but God is the Strength of my Heart, and my Portion for ever;* *Pfal.* 73. 25, 26. Then pray hard for the Sealings and Witnefs of the Spirit; beg the Lord, with *Auftin,* to fay unto thy Soul, *I am thy Salvation.*

4. Would you indeed live at Reft in God? Then meditate and contemplate him much, dwell much in the View of his Glorious Excellencies and Perfections: Deep and frequent Meditation of God and his Excellencies does marveoufly endear God unto Souls, and withal brings them into an Acquaintance with thofe fatisfying Delights that are to be found in him, and fo to a Reft in him. *My Soul, (fays David) fhall be fatisfied as with Marrow and Fatnefs, and my Mouth fhall praife thee with joyful Lips, when I remember thee upon my Bed, and meditate on thee in the Night-watches,* Pfal. 63. 5, 6. In *Verf.* 3. he is even ravifhed with the Senfe and Incomes of God's Love to him: *Thy Loving kindnefs is better than Life, my Lips fhall praife thee;* and here he fpeaks of Satisfaction, the fweeteft Satisfaction, and all that which came in a Way of Holy Meditation; and again, *my Meditation of thee fhall be fweet,* Pfal. 104. 34. Holy Meditation of God produces many fweet Experiences of God in the

Soul,

Soul, Experiences of his Grace, of his Love, of his Sweetnefs, of the Bleffednefs of Communion with him, and the like; and thefe Experiences iffue in the Soul's Reft in him: Every new Experience of God draws the Heart further into God, and makes it center more in him: Every Tafte, every Sight, of God, every new Emanation of his Glory before the Soul, (of which in the Holy Meditation of God the Saints have'not a few) weans and works the Heart off from carnal, fenfible, things, and makes him to cleave more clofely and entirely to God, gathering in about him as his All. O, be much in the Meditation of God: 'Tis not enough for us to know him, and to know him in Chrift; no, nor to know him as ours, as our God in Covenant, but we muft ftudy him; we muft meditate what a God he is, and fingle him out, now under one, and then under another, Notion or Confideration, to meditate upon, begging God to help us in our Meditations of him. The moft know and enjoy little of God, becaufe they meditate him fo little, they are little in Holy Meditation.

5. Would you indeed be at Reft in God? Then improve all your Experiences of the Creatures Vanity, for the carrying of your Souls more into God, as your Reft and Centre. Holy *David* did fo, and 'tis indeed a great Piece of a Chriftian's Skill. *Pfal.* 39. 7. *And now, Lord,* (fays he) *what wait I for? My Hope is in thee:* If you view either the foregoing or following Part of the *Pfalm*, you will find that *David* was under great Experiences of the Creatures Vanity, he faw the Vanity of worldly Enjoyments, they are all *but a vain Show*, he faw his own Vanity, he faw the Vanity of others, he found every one, and every thing, nothing but Vanity, and what is the Iffue? What Ufe does he make of it? This, he gathers in

more

more to God as his only Reft and Happinefs, *Now, Lord, what want I for? My Hope is in thee;* q. d. Now I have done with the Creatures, I fee what they are, and what all Perfons and Things are, and I have done with all, thou thy felf only, O Lord, art my Reft, my Happinefs, my All. Thus when at any time you meet with frefh Experiences of the Creatures Vanity, improve them for the carrying of your Souls more in to God, as your Reft. You fcarce live that Day wherein you do not meet with new Experiences of the Creatures Vanity, this is loft, and that is imbittered, to you; now you meet with Difappointments, and then with Sorrows, Wounds, and Snares; and that, where it may be, you expected your Chief Comfort and Satisfaction, now in all fuch Cafes what fhould we do? Retire the more into God, as our Reft and Happinefs: Say with the *Pfalmift, Now, Lord, what want I for? My Hope is in thee,* I have done with the Streams, I'll cleave only to thee, the Fountain, the Creatures ever ferve me thus, they leave me under Sorrows, Snares, and Difappointments, thou, Lord, fhalt be all in all to me, thou art my only Reft for ever.

6. Would you indeed live at Reft in God? Then pray for much Spirituality of Heart, much Suitednefs of Spirit to God and Chrift. The more Spiritual you are, the more are you fuited to the Bleffed God, and the more you are fuited to G d, the more fully and genuinely will your Souls reft in him. I fuppofe you have a new Heart, (for I fpeak unto you as to Saints) the old Heart to be fure will never reft in God, the old Heart is wholly averfe from God, and at Enmi y with him, it hates him, 'tis wholly carnal, fenfual, and unclean, and delights only in things fuitable to it felf: Let all therefore that would reft in God, firft get a new Heart, fuch as God promifes in his Covenant, *Ezek.* 36. 26. and having gotten a new Heart, pray
for

for much Spirituality of Heart and Affection Alas! Alas! We are *carnal,* (as *Paul* charged his *Corinthians*) and being carnal, we lean to, and hanker after, carnal things, and till we get more Spirituality, we ſhall not reſt ſo fully in God as we ſhould; therefore pray unto God hard for more of this, pray for more of his Spirit to act and influence you; and not only ſo, but to change you more and more into the Divine Life and Image.

To conclude all; Live at Reſt all that ever you can in God here, but withal look, and long, and haſten, to that Reſt which remains for Saints with God in the other World: True Reſt in God here is ſweet, but we ſhall never be fully and perfectly Happy till we enter that future Reſt: That indeed carries a compleat Happineſs in it; O, to be wholly ſwallowed up in the Divine Will, the Divine Life, the Divine Fulneſs, the Ocean of Divine Love, to have every Faculty, and every Affection, perfectly ſuited to God, and filled with God, this cannot but be perfect Reſt and Happineſs; eſpecially conſidering what an Enlargement there will be of all the Faculties, and how much of God they will then take in: But till we reach this Reſt we cannot have any compleat Reſt; therefore breathe and ſuſpire after the future Reſt, keep your Eye much there, and let your Eye affect your Heart; look and love, love and long, long and haſten to that Sweet, that Holy, that Heavenly, that Inviolable, that Unchangeable and Eternal, Reſt which remains for Saints in God and with God in the other World, crying out, both in your Spirits and Lives, *Come, Lord Jeſus, come quickly.* Amen.

F I N I S.